Dedication

Dedicated to all drivers who navigate roads, waters, and skies with skill, diligence, and dedication, shaping the fabric of transportation and connectivity worldwide.

Table of Contents

Chapter 1. Introduction
Chapter 2. Agriculture Vehicles
Chapter 3. Ambulance Drivers
Chapter 4. Armored Car Drivers
Chapter 5. Bus Drivers
Chapter 6. Chauffeurs
Chapter 7. Construction Vehicles
Chapter 8. Courier and Messenger Drivers
Chapter 9. Delivery Drivers
Chapter 10. Driving School Instructors
Chapter 11. Emergency Vehicle Drivers
Chapter 12. Forklift Operators
Chapter 13. Garbage Truck Drivers
Chapter 14. Heavy Equipment Operators
Chapter 15. Ice Cream Truck Drivers
Chapter 16. Limousine Drivers
Chapter 17. Mail Carriers
Chapter 18. Metro (Subway) Operators
Chapter 19. Military Vehicle Drivers
Chapter 20. Motorcycle Couriers
Chapter 21. Paratransit Drivers
Chapter 22. Police Car Drivers
Chapter 23. Private Hire Drivers
Chapter 24. Public Transportation Drivers
Chapter 25. Racing Drivers
Chapter 26. Ride-Hailing Drivers
Chapter 27. Roadside Assistance Services
Chapter 28. School Bus Drivers
Chapter 29. Sightseeing Tour Bus Drivers
Chapter 30. Taxi Drivers
Chapter 31. Tow Truck Operators
Chapter 32. Train Drivers
Chapter 33. Tram Drivers
Chapter 34. Truck (Lorry) Drivers
Chapter 35. Valet Drivers
Chapter 36. Watercraft Drivers
Chapter 37. Wildlife Park Safari Drivers

Chapter 1. Introduction

Driving is not merely a method of transportation; it is a cornerstone of modern society, facilitating the movement of people, goods, and services across vast distances and through bustling urban centers. At its core, driving as a job and profession encompasses a diverse array of roles, each characterized by its own unique challenges, responsibilities, and intrinsic rewards. It is a profession that blends practical skills with profound societal impact.

In today's interconnected world, drivers serve as essential conduits of commerce and community. From the dedicated school bus driver ensuring the safe transport of children to their educational destinations, to the meticulous courier navigating city streets to deliver packages on time, to the skilled emergency medical technician racing against time to provide life-saving care—each driver plays a pivotal role in maintaining the rhythm of daily life. They embody reliability and responsibility on the road.

The profession of driving demands a blend of technical expertise, situational awareness, and interpersonal skills. Drivers must master the intricacies of vehicle operation, from the mechanics of acceleration and braking to the nuances of navigating diverse terrain and weather conditions. They are adept at utilizing advanced technologies such as GPS navigation systems, route optimization software, and vehicle diagnostic tools to enhance efficiency and safety on the road. Continuous adaptation to new technologies is key to staying ahead in the field.

Navigating the regulatory landscape is also integral to the role of a professional driver. Licensing requirements, safety regulations, and compliance with industry standards ensure that drivers operate within legal boundaries while upholding high standards of safety and professionalism. Continuous training and professional development are essential to staying abreast of evolving regulations and industry best practices, ensuring drivers remain at the forefront of their profession.

The challenges encountered by drivers are as diverse as the environments they traverse. Long-haul truck drivers endure extended periods away from home, managing fatigue and loneliness while maintaining strict delivery schedules and adhering to federal hours-of-service regulations. Taxi and rideshare drivers navigate congested city streets, responding to dynamic passenger demands while managing the pressures of peak-hour traffic and fluctuating fares. Each journey presents its own unique set of obstacles and opportunities for growth.

Emergency vehicle drivers operate under intense pressure, making split-second decisions in high-stakes situations to ensure the timely arrival of critical services. They must navigate through traffic with speed and precision while coordinating closely with dispatchers and emergency response teams to deliver swift and effective assistance to those in need. Their role demands not only technical skill but also a cool-headed demeanor and unwavering dedication to public safety.

In addition to technical skills and regulatory knowledge, driving as a profession requires a profound commitment to customer service and community engagement. Drivers often serve as ambassadors for their respective organizations, providing a friendly face and a reassuring presence to passengers and clients. They develop strong interpersonal skills to handle diverse customer interactions and to address concerns with empathy and professionalism, fostering trust and loyalty among their clientele.

Technological advancements continue to shape the landscape of driving professions. The integration of telematics systems allows fleet managers to monitor driver behavior and vehicle performance in real-time, promoting safer driving practices and optimizing operational efficiency. Autonomous vehicle technology promises to revolutionize the industry, raising questions about the future roles and responsibilities of drivers in an increasingly automated world. Adaptation to technological changes ensures drivers remain at the forefront of industry advancements.

Despite the challenges and technological advancements, driving remains a deeply human endeavor. Drivers witness the ebb and flow of daily life, from the joyous moments of families reuniting at airports to the solemnity of delivering supplies to communities affected by natural disasters. They forge connections with passengers and clients, offering comfort during difficult journeys and celebrating milestones along the way. Their role extends beyond transportation; it is about providing essential services and making meaningful contributions to society.

Explore the world of driving as both a job and a profession. Discover driving as a serious yet fascinating means of earning a living. Learn about the challenges drivers face and how to grow from them, the regulations that maintain order, and the significant work and responsibility drivers shoulder in their roles. Join us as we journey down less-traveled roads and uncover various aspects of this profession to make the most of this experience together.

Chapter 2: Agriculture Vehicles

Agriculture is an important part of any economy. A country cannot be self-sufficient in terms of food needs without the success of its agricultural sector. Agricultural vehicles play an important role from plantation to harvest.

Roles and Responsibilities

Agricultural vehicle operators undertake critical roles in the farming industry, encompassing a wide array of tasks essential for crop cultivation and management. Tractor drivers, for instance, are responsible for soil preparation, plowing, and seeding, ensuring optimal conditions for crop growth. Combine operators oversee harvesting operations, meticulously gathering and processing crops to maximize yield and quality. Throughout the agricultural cycle, equipment handlers maintain and operate specialized machinery, from sprayers to balers, contributing to efficient farm operations.

Daily Operations

The daily routines of agricultural vehicle operators revolve around seasonal demands and crop cycles. During planting season, operators meticulously calibrate seed drills and monitor planting depth to ensure uniform seed distribution. Throughout the growing season, they engage in tasks such as fertilization, pest control, and irrigation, all while maneuvering heavy equipment over challenging terrain. Harvesting involves precise timing and coordination as operators navigate fields to gather mature crops efficiently, often working long hours to capitalize on optimal weather conditions.

Challenges

Agricultural driving presents unique challenges rooted in the nature of farm work and rural environments. Operators must adeptly navigate diverse terrain, including steep slopes, muddy fields, and narrow pathways between crop rows. The size and weight of agricultural machinery demand careful maneuvering and heightened awareness to prevent damage to crops and equipment alike. Adverse weather conditions, from sudden storms to sweltering heat, further complicate operations, requiring operators to adapt swiftly and prioritize safety and productivity.

Safety Considerations
Safety is paramount in agricultural driving, where operators contend with hazards ranging from equipment malfunctions to unpredictable wildlife encounters. Rigorous adherence to safety protocols is essential, including regular maintenance checks to ensure machinery operates at peak performance. Operators equip themselves with personal protective gear and utilize advanced safety features such as rollover protection systems (ROPS) and seat belts to mitigate risks. Training programs emphasize safe operating practices and emergency procedures to safeguard both operators and bystanders on and off the farm.

Technological Advancements
Technological innovations are transforming agricultural vehicles, enhancing efficiency, precision, and sustainability in farm operations. GPS-guided tractors and combines enable operators to execute field tasks with unprecedented accuracy, minimizing overlap and optimizing fuel usage. Automated systems for planting, fertilizing, and harvesting streamline operations, reducing labor demands and increasing productivity. Precision farming techniques leverage data analytics and remote sensing technologies to monitor crop health and optimize resource allocation, promoting sustainable agricultural practices.

Environmental Concerns

Agricultural vehicles are essential to modern farming practices, but their operation can significantly affect environmental sustainability. Efforts to reduce carbon footprints and minimize resource consumption are increasingly prioritized through advancements in fuel efficiency and emissions control technologies. Sustainable farming practices, such as conservation tillage and integrated pest management, complement technological innovations to promote soil health and biodiversity conservation. Agricultural vehicle operators are integral to implementing these practices, contributing to environmental stewardship and long-term agricultural sustainability.

Regulatory Landscape
Operating agricultural vehicles requires compliance with a complex regulatory framework aimed at ensuring safety, environmental protection, and fair labor practices. Licensing requirements vary by jurisdiction, with operators often required to obtain commercial driver's licenses (CDLs) or specialized endorsements based on equipment size and payload capacities. Regulatory oversight extends to equipment standards, emissions regulations, and workplace safety guidelines, underscoring the importance of ongoing training and adherence to industry standards.

Career Paths and Opportunities
Driving in agriculture presents a range of career paths with opportunities for advancement and specialization within the farming industry. Seasonal employment is common during peak planting and harvesting seasons, providing flexibility for operators to pursue additional training or education during off-peak periods. Advancements in technology and mechanization present opportunities for skilled operators to transition into roles as equipment technicians, farm managers, or agricultural consultants. Professional development programs and industry certifications are instrumental in supporting career advancement in agriculture,

providing operators with essential skills and knowledge to thrive in dynamic agricultural environments.

Community and Industry Relations

Agricultural vehicle operators play a vital role in rural communities, supporting local economies and fostering collaborative relationships within the farming industry. Beyond their operational roles, operators engage in community outreach initiatives and educational programs to promote agricultural literacy and sustainability. Industry associations and cooperatives provide networking opportunities and advocacy platforms, empowering operators to influence agricultural policies and contribute to the collective advancement of farming practices.

Chapter 3. Ambulance Drivers

Ambulance drivers play an essential role in emergency medical services (EMS), providing critical care and transportation to patients in need. Their commitment to patient safety, adherence to regulatory standards, and dedication to community health contribute to the effectiveness and resilience of healthcare systems worldwide. Through their personal perspectives and professional experiences, ambulance drivers inspire appreciation and recognition for their invaluable contributions to public health and safety.

Roles and Responsibilities
Ambulance drivers play a critical role in the emergency medical services (EMS) system, serving as the frontline operators responsible for transporting patients safely and swiftly to medical facilities. Their primary responsibility is to ensure that patients receive timely and efficient transport while maintaining their stability and comfort during transit. Ambulance drivers work closely with paramedics and emergency medical technicians (EMTs), who provide medical care and treatment to patients en route to hospitals or other healthcare facilities.

In addition to driving, ambulance drivers are responsible for a range of essential tasks. They must maintain constant communication with dispatch centers to receive emergency calls and coordinate their responses effectively. This communication is vital for receiving information about the nature of the emergency, the location of the incident, and any specific medical needs of the patient. Ambulance drivers also play a crucial role in ensuring the ambulance is properly stocked and equipped with necessary medical supplies and equipment, such as stretchers, oxygen tanks, and basic life support (BLS) tools.

Ambulance drivers are trained to navigate various environments and road conditions, from congested urban streets to remote rural areas. They must possess excellent driving skills and a thorough knowledge of local roads and traffic patterns to minimize response times and ensure the safety of both the crew and the patient. During emergencies, drivers must make quick decisions under pressure, such as choosing the fastest and safest route to the hospital or providing immediate assistance to stabilize a patient's condition.

Daily Operations
The daily operations of ambulance drivers are characterized by unpredictability and urgency. Shifts can vary widely in terms of workload and intensity, depending on factors such as the volume of emergency calls, the severity of incidents, and external conditions like weather or traffic congestion. Ambulance drivers typically work in shifts that can span 8 to 12 hours or more, including evenings, weekends, and holidays, to ensure round-the-clock availability of emergency medical services.

A typical day for an ambulance driver begins with a thorough inspection and maintenance check of the ambulance and its equipment. This includes ensuring that all medical supplies are stocked, the ambulance is fueled and mechanically sound, and communication systems are operational. Ambulance drivers often start their shifts by reviewing the day's schedule, including scheduled hospital transfers, standby duties, and any ongoing incidents or emergencies in their assigned area.

Once on duty, ambulance drivers must be prepared to respond to emergency calls at a moment's notice. When responding to a call, emergency responders must promptly evaluate the situation, gather crucial details from dispatchers, and swiftly navigate to the incident location. This process requires drivers to maintain composure and focus while driving under potentially stressful conditions, such as maneuvering through heavy traffic or adverse weather.

During patient transport, ambulance drivers work closely with paramedics and EMTs to ensure the patient's safety and comfort. They may assist in lifting and transferring patients on stretchers, securing them in the ambulance, and providing reassurance and support during transit. Ambulance drivers must adhere to strict protocols for patient care and transport, including maintaining patient confidentiality and ensuring compliance with medical directives provided by healthcare professionals.

Challenges
Ambulance driving presents a unique set of challenges that require drivers to adapt quickly and perform effectively under pressure. One of the primary challenges is navigating through congested traffic and unpredictable road conditions while responding to emergency calls. In urban areas, drivers must contend with heavy traffic, road closures, and construction zones, which can significantly impact response times and patient outcomes.

Another challenge ambulance drivers face is the need to maintain situational awareness and make critical decisions in high-stress environments. During emergencies, drivers must assess the severity of patients' conditions, prioritize medical interventions, and communicate effectively with paramedics and healthcare professionals. They must also ensure the safety of themselves, their crew members, and other road users while driving at high speeds and maneuvering through challenging terrain.

Ambulance drivers also encounter challenges related to patient care and management during transit. They may transport patients with varying medical conditions, from minor injuries to life-threatening emergencies, requiring drivers to adapt their driving techniques and provide appropriate support and reassurance. Maintaining patient stability and comfort during transport is essential, requiring drivers to monitor vital signs, administer basic medical interventions as needed, and communicate effectively with paramedics to ensure continuity of care.

Safety Considerations
Safety is a paramount concern for ambulance drivers, who operate under demanding conditions that require a high level of skill, training, and situational awareness. Ambulance drivers undergo specialized training in defensive driving techniques, emergency vehicle operations, and patient handling to mitigate risks and ensure the safety of patients, crew members, and the public.

One of the key safety considerations for ambulance drivers is maintaining control and stability of the ambulance while responding to emergency calls. Ambulances are equipped with advanced safety features such as anti-lock braking systems (ABS), electronic stability control (ESC), and traction control systems (TCS) to enhance vehicle stability and maneuverability in challenging road conditions.

Ambulance drivers must also adhere to strict protocols for infection control and patient safety during transport. They are trained to use personal protective equipment (PPE), such as gloves, masks, and gowns, to prevent the spread of infectious diseases and maintain a sterile environment within the ambulance. Maintaining proper hand hygiene and following disinfection procedures are critical to reducing the risk of cross-contamination and ensuring the safety of both patients and crew members.

In addition to driving safely, ambulance drivers must be prepared to handle medical emergencies and provide immediate assistance to patients in critical condition. They receive training in basic life support (BLS) techniques, including cardiopulmonary resuscitation (CPR), airway management, and bleeding control, to stabilize patients' conditions until they reach a medical facility.

Technological Advancements
Technological advancements have revolutionized ambulance operations, enhancing efficiency, communication, and patient care outcomes. GPS navigation systems play a crucial role in route planning and navigation, allowing drivers to identify the fastest and safest routes to emergency scenes and medical facilities. Real-time traffic updates and rerouting capabilities enable drivers to avoid congestion and reduce response times, improving overall service delivery.

Ambulances are equipped with advanced communication systems that enable seamless communication between drivers, dispatchers, paramedics, and healthcare facilities. These systems facilitate the transmission of vital information, such as patient demographics, medical history, and vital signs, to ensure continuity of care and informed decision-making during transport.

Onboard medical equipment and technology enable ambulance drivers to provide immediate medical interventions and support to patients en route to hospitals. Ambulances are equipped with cardiac monitors, defibrillators, intravenous (IV) therapy equipment, and advanced airway management devices to stabilize patients' conditions and manage medical emergencies effectively.

Vehicle telemetry systems monitor ambulance performance and diagnostics in real-time, alerting drivers to potential issues such as engine malfunctions or mechanical failures. This proactive approach to vehicle maintenance ensures ambulance readiness and reliability, minimizes downtime, and optimizes operational efficiency.

Environmental Impact

Ambulance services are increasingly focused on minimizing their environmental impact through sustainable practices and technology adoption. Ambulances are equipped with fuel-efficient engines and emission control systems to reduce carbon emissions and air pollutants during operations. Hybrid and electric ambulance models are being explored as alternatives to traditional diesel-powered vehicles, offering lower emissions and reduced fuel consumption.

In addition to vehicle technology, ambulance services implement eco-friendly practices such as idle reduction strategies and energy-efficient lighting and equipment. These initiatives not only reduce environmental impact but also lower operating costs and promote sustainability within healthcare organizations.

Ambulance drivers play a role in promoting environmental stewardship by advocating for sustainable practices and participating in training programs on eco-friendly driving techniques. By prioritizing fuel efficiency, emission reduction, and environmental responsibility, ambulance services contribute to global efforts to mitigate climate change and promote a healthier environment for communities.

Regulatory Landscape

Ambulance drivers operate within a complex regulatory framework that governs emergency medical services (EMS) and ensures adherence to standards of care, patient safety, and operational efficiency. Regulatory requirements vary by jurisdiction but generally include licensing, certification, and ongoing training for ambulance personnel to maintain competency and compliance with evolving industry standards.

Ambulance drivers are typically required to hold a valid commercial driver's license (CDL) with endorsements for operating emergency vehicles. They must also complete specialized training and certification programs in emergency vehicle operations, defensive driving, and medical transport to ensure safe and effective service delivery.

Regulatory agencies establish standards for ambulance equipment, vehicle maintenance, and infection control to uphold patient safety and operational readiness. Ambulance services undergo regular inspections and audits to assess compliance with regulatory requirements and identify areas for improvement in service delivery and patient care.

Continuous education and professional development are integral to maintaining regulatory compliance and enhancing ambulance drivers' skills and knowledge. Training programs cover a wide range of topics, including CPR certification renewal, advanced life support (ALS) protocols, and updates on regulatory changes affecting EMS operations.

Career Paths and Opportunities
Ambulance driving offers diverse career paths within the healthcare sector, providing opportunities for professional growth, specialization, and advancement in emergency medical services (EMS). Ambulance drivers may pursue careers as paramedics, emergency medical technicians (EMTs), or advanced practice providers (APPs) by obtaining additional education, training, and certification in specialized areas of medical care.

Professional development programs and continuing education opportunities enable ambulance drivers to expand their clinical skills, enhance patient care abilities, and pursue certifications in advanced life support (ALS), pediatric emergency care, or trauma management. These credentials enhance career prospects and qualify drivers for leadership roles in EMS administration, education, or specialized medical transport services.

Ambulance services may offer career advancement opportunities through promotional pathways, such as supervisory positions, shift leadership roles, or specialized assignments in critical care transport (CCT) or air medical services (AMS). Leadership training programs prepare ambulance drivers for managerial responsibilities, including staff supervision, budget management, and strategic planning in healthcare settings.

Ambulance drivers contribute to the healthcare workforce by delivering essential emergency medical services and supporting patient care initiatives in their communities. Emergency medical responders play a vital role in public health and safety by promptly responding to medical emergencies, administering critical care interventions, and fostering community health awareness through outreach and education initiatives.

Community Engagement

Ambulance drivers are integral to community health and safety initiatives, collaborating with healthcare providers, emergency responders, and community organizations to enhance emergency preparedness and response. They participate in public education campaigns, community events, and health fairs to raise awareness about CPR training, injury prevention, and emergency medical services (EMS) resources available to residents.

Ambulance drivers engage with diverse community stakeholders to build partnerships and strengthen relationships that support effective emergency response and patient care delivery. They participate in interdisciplinary teams, including disaster response task forces, community health coalitions, and public safety committees, to coordinate emergency preparedness efforts and promote resilience in local communities.

Public outreach initiatives led by ambulance drivers include CPR training workshops, first aid demonstrations, and safety presentations tailored to community groups, schools, and civic organizations. These educational efforts empower community members to take proactive steps in emergency situations, such as calling 911 promptly, administering basic life support (BLS) interventions, and supporting individuals in medical distress until professional help arrives.

Ambulance drivers serve as ambassadors for emergency medical services (EMS), advocating for public health initiatives, injury prevention strategies, and community-based healthcare services. They foster trust and confidence in ambulance services by demonstrating professionalism, compassion, and commitment to delivering high-quality patient care during critical incidents and medical emergencies.

Chapter 4. Armored Car Drivers

Armored car drivers play an essential role in secure transport services, ensuring the safe and efficient delivery of valuable goods while maintaining rigorous security protocols and regulatory compliance. Through their dedication, vigilance, and professionalism, armored car drivers uphold the integrity of the transportation industry and support the operational needs of businesses and financial institutions worldwide.

Roles and Responsibilities
Armored car drivers are pivotal in the secure transport of valuable goods such as cash, jewelry, and other high-value items. They ensure the safe and reliable delivery of these assets, employing rigorous security protocols and adherence to strict operational procedures. Their primary responsibility is to ensure the safe and timely delivery of these assets between locations such as banks, businesses, and ATMs. Armored car drivers are entrusted with maintaining the security and integrity of the cargo throughout the transport process, adhering to strict protocols to prevent theft or loss.

Daily Operations
The daily operations of armored car drivers are centered around the secure handling and transport of valuable goods. Each day begins with thorough vehicle inspections to ensure the armored car is in optimal condition for transport. Drivers must verify the integrity of security features such as bullet-resistant glass, reinforced doors, and locking mechanisms before loading valuables into the vehicle.

Once on duty, armored car drivers receive detailed manifests outlining the specific items to be transported and the designated delivery locations. They may be responsible for multiple stops throughout their shift, requiring efficient route planning and adherence to strict schedules to meet delivery deadlines while maintaining security protocols.

During transport, armored car drivers must remain vigilant and alert to potential security threats or suspicious activities. They utilize defensive driving techniques and maintain situational awareness to reduce risks and prioritize the safety of themselves, their crew members, and their valuable cargo. In the event of an emergency or security breach, drivers are trained to follow established procedures for contacting law enforcement and responding to threats.

Security Protocols
Security is paramount in armored car operations, with drivers trained extensively in security protocols and emergency procedures. They undergo rigorous background checks and security clearances before employment and receive specialized training in defensive driving, firearms handling (where permitted), and crisis management to handle potential threats effectively.

Armored car drivers are equipped with communication devices to maintain contact with dispatch centers and law enforcement agencies during transport. They follow strict procedures for securing and transporting valuable items, including the use of armored containers, tamper-evident seals, and GPS tracking systems to monitor the location and status of the cargo in real-time.

Challenges
Armored car drivers face unique challenges related to the nature of their work and the valuable cargo they transport. They operate

in diverse environments, ranging from urban centers with heavy traffic to remote areas with limited infrastructure, requiring adaptability and problem-solving skills to navigate varying conditions safely.

One of the primary challenges for armored car drivers is maintaining vigilance against potential security threats, such as robbery attempts or ambushes. They must be prepared to respond calmly and decisively to emergencies while prioritizing the safety of themselves and others involved.

Additionally, armored car drivers must contend with the physical demands of the job, including lifting and moving heavy containers of currency or valuables. They may work long hours, including nights, weekends, and holidays, to ensure continuous coverage and meet the demands of clients and businesses relying on secure transport services.

Technological Integration
Advancements in technology play a crucial role in enhancing the efficiency and security of armored car operations. GPS tracking systems enable real-time monitoring of vehicle locations and routes, allowing dispatch centers to optimize route planning and respond quickly to unforeseen circumstances or emergencies.

Armored cars are equipped with state-of-the-art security features, including surveillance cameras, panic alarms, and encrypted communication systems, to safeguard against theft and unauthorized access. These technologies provide drivers with enhanced situational awareness and support law enforcement agencies in investigating security incidents.

Regulatory Compliance
Armored car drivers must adhere to strict regulatory standards governing the secure transport of valuables and the operation of

armored vehicles. Regulatory requirements vary by jurisdiction but typically include licensing, certification, and ongoing training to ensure compliance with industry-specific regulations and security protocols.

Drivers undergo periodic inspections and audits to verify the integrity of security measures and adherence to operational standards. They are responsible for maintaining accurate records of transport activities, including manifests, delivery receipts, and incident reports, to document the chain of custody and ensure accountability in the handling of valuable items.

Career Paths and Opportunities

A career as an armored car driver offers opportunities for professional growth and advancement within the security and transportation industries. Experienced drivers may pursue leadership roles in security operations, logistics management, or specialized services such as executive protection or secure asset management.

Professional development programs provide armored car drivers with opportunities to enhance their skills in security management, risk assessment, and crisis response. Certifications in security management, firearms proficiency, and emergency preparedness prepare drivers for leadership positions and specialized assignments requiring advanced knowledge and expertise.

Community Engagement

Armored car drivers contribute to community safety by ensuring the secure transport of valuable goods and supporting businesses and financial institutions in their daily operations. They collaborate with law enforcement agencies and security professionals to promote crime prevention initiatives and enhance public safety awareness in their communities.

Drivers participate in community outreach programs, security seminars, and educational workshops to educate businesses and the public about effective security practices and the importance of secure transport services. Their engagement fosters partnerships with local stakeholders and enhances the resilience of businesses against potential security threats.

Chapter 5. Bus Drivers

Bus drivers play a vital role in public transportation systems, delivering safe, reliable, and efficient transportation services to passengers. Through their dedication, professionalism, and commitment to passenger safety and customer service, bus drivers contribute to the mobility, accessibility, and sustainability of communities worldwide.

Roles and Responsibilities
Bus drivers fulfill a pivotal role in public transportation systems, responsible for safely transporting passengers along designated routes. Their primary responsibility is to ensure the safety and comfort of passengers while adhering to traffic laws, schedules, and operational guidelines. Bus drivers play a critical role in maintaining efficient and reliable transportation services and providing essential mobility options for commuters, students, and the general public.

Daily Operations
The daily operations of bus drivers encompass a variety of tasks aimed at delivering safe and dependable transportation services. Each day begins with pre-trip inspections of the bus to verify mechanical integrity, safety features, and cleanliness. Drivers check essential components such as brakes, tires, lights, and emergency exits to ensure compliance with safety regulations and optimal performance.

Once on duty, bus drivers review their assigned routes and schedules, coordinating with dispatchers or transit authorities to receive updates on traffic conditions, route changes, or special instructions. They greet passengers courteously, assist with boarding and fare collection, and provide information about routes, stops, and connections to ensure a positive customer experience.

During transit, bus drivers must maintain focus and concentration while operating large vehicles in varying traffic and weather conditions. They exercise defensive driving techniques to anticipate and react to potential hazards, such as sudden stops, pedestrian crossings, and inclement weather, to ensure passenger safety and operational efficiency.

Passenger Safety and Assistance

Ensuring passenger safety is paramount for bus drivers, who are trained to handle emergencies and provide assistance as needed. They enforce safety regulations, such as seatbelt use and prohibitions on smoking or disruptive behavior, to maintain a secure environment for all passengers. Bus drivers receive training in emergency procedures, including evacuations, first aid, and communication protocols, to respond effectively to incidents on board.

Bus drivers assist passengers with disabilities or special needs, ensuring accessibility and accommodation in accordance with the Americans with Disabilities Act (ADA) or local accessibility standards. They may deploy wheelchair lifts or ramps, secure mobility devices, and provide guidance or support to passengers with limited mobility to facilitate safe boarding and disembarking.

Route Management and Efficiency

Efficient route management is essential for bus drivers to adhere to schedules and minimize delays while providing reliable transportation services. They navigate designated routes, making scheduled stops at designated bus stops or transit stations to pick up and drop off passengers according to established timetables. Bus drivers adjust their driving speed and adherence to traffic signals and regulations to maintain schedule adherence and passenger comfort.

Bus drivers monitor vehicle performance and fuel consumption, reporting any mechanical issues or maintenance needs to maintenance staff or supervisors promptly. They contribute to the efficient operation of public transportation systems by optimizing route efficiency, reducing fuel consumption, and promoting sustainability through eco-friendly driving practices.

Customer Service and Communication

Bus drivers play a vital role in customer service, interacting with passengers professionally and courteously throughout their journey. They provide information about fares, routes, schedules, and destinations to assist passengers in planning their trips effectively. Bus drivers address passenger inquiries, concerns, or complaints promptly, resolving issues and ensuring a positive customer experience.

Effective communication skills are essential for bus drivers to convey important information to passengers, such as upcoming stops, route changes, or service disruptions. They announce stops and transfer points clearly, using public address systems or visual displays to keep passengers informed and engaged during their journey. Bus drivers maintain continuous communication with dispatchers or transit control centers to report operational issues, coordinate service adjustments, and promptly request assistance when needed. This communication ensures efficient and safe transit operations for passengers and personnel alike.

Challenges

Bus drivers encounter various challenges in their daily work, ranging from traffic congestion and inclement weather to passenger behavior and safety concerns. They must navigate crowded streets, construction zones, and unpredictable road conditions while maintaining schedule adherence and passenger comfort. Bus drivers exercise patience and professionalism to manage challenging situations, such as route deviations, vehicle breakdowns, or disruptive behavior, to ensure safe and efficient transportation services.

Technological Integration
Technological advancements play a significant role in enhancing the efficiency, safety, and sustainability of bus transportation systems. Bus drivers utilize onboard technology, such as GPS navigation systems and automated vehicle location (AVL) systems, to optimize route planning, monitor real-time traffic conditions, and adjust schedules dynamically. These technologies improve operational efficiency, reduce fuel consumption, and enhance passenger satisfaction by minimizing wait times and travel delays.

Regulatory Compliance
Bus drivers operate within a regulatory framework that governs public transportation services, ensuring compliance with safety standards, operational guidelines, and passenger rights. They hold commercial driver's licenses (CDL) with endorsements for passenger transport, requiring specialized training and certification in defensive driving, passenger safety, and emergency procedures. Bus drivers undergo regular medical examinations and background checks to maintain eligibility for operating commercial vehicles and ensure passenger safety.

Career Paths and Opportunities
A career as a bus driver offers opportunities for professional growth and advancement within the public transportation industry. Experienced drivers may pursue supervisory roles, such as route supervisors or transportation managers, responsible for overseeing operational efficiency, staff training, and customer service initiatives. Professional development programs and continuing education opportunities enable bus drivers to enhance their skills in leadership, management, and transit operations,

preparing them for career advancement and leadership roles in public transportation agencies or private transit companies.

Community Engagement

Bus drivers engage with the community by providing essential transportation services and raising public awareness about transit options and resources. They participate in community outreach programs, safety initiatives, and educational campaigns to promote sustainable transportation practices, enhance passenger safety, and improve public transit accessibility. Bus drivers collaborate with local stakeholders, community organizations, and government agencies to address transportation needs, support economic development, and strengthen community connections through accessible and reliable public transportation services.

Chapter 6. Chauffeurs

Chauffeurs play an essential role in providing personalized transportation services, delivering exceptional hospitality, and ensuring safe and comfortable travel experiences for clients. Through their professionalism, attention to detail, and commitment to service excellence, chauffeurs contribute to the success and reputation of private transportation providers and enhance the overall travel experience for clients worldwide.

Roles and Responsibilities

Chauffeurs play a crucial role in delivering personalized transportation services to clients, ensuring their travel experiences are safe, comfortable, and tailored to their needs. Their primary responsibility is to chauffeur clients to their destinations in a timely and professional manner, offering door-to-door service and maintaining a high standard of hospitality and discretion. Chauffeurs cater to the unique preferences and needs of clients, delivering exceptional service while adhering to traffic laws and safety regulations.

Client Service and Hospitality

Chauffeurs excel in client service and hospitality, creating a welcoming and accommodating environment for passengers throughout their journey. They greet clients courteously, assist with luggage handling, and provide information about local attractions, dining options, and points of interest. Chauffeurs anticipate client needs, offering amenities such as bottled water, reading materials, or mobile device chargers to enhance comfort and convenience during travel.

Vehicle Maintenance and Care

Maintaining the cleanliness and mechanical integrity of the vehicle is essential for chauffeurs to ensure safe and reliable transportation services. They perform daily vehicle inspections, checking fluid levels, tire pressure, and overall condition to ensure optimal performance and passenger safety. Chauffeurs coordinate regular maintenance and repairs with trusted service providers to uphold vehicle reliability and presentation standards.

Route Planning and Navigation

Efficient route planning and navigation skills are critical for chauffeurs to optimize travel routes, minimize delays, and ensure punctual arrivals at destinations. They rely on GPS navigation systems and real-time traffic updates to navigate through traffic patterns, handle road closures, and find alternative routes efficiently. Chauffeurs adapt their driving strategies to changing conditions, prioritizing passenger comfort and safety while maintaining schedule adherence.

Professionalism and Discretion

Chauffeurs maintain a high level of professionalism and discretion in all interactions with clients, respecting privacy and confidentiality at all times. They uphold ethical standards and confidentiality agreements, safeguarding client information and personal belongings entrusted during travel. Chauffeurs exhibit impeccable grooming, attire, and communication skills to convey professionalism and build trust with clients.

Safety and Emergency Preparedness

Ensuring passenger safety is paramount for chauffeurs, who undergo specialized training in defensive driving techniques, emergency procedures, and crisis management. They remain vigilant and alert to potential hazards, such as adverse weather conditions, erratic drivers, or pedestrian crossings, to mitigate risks and ensure a safe travel environment. Chauffeurs are proficient in first aid and CPR, prepared to respond promptly to medical emergencies or roadside incidents.

Etiquette and Protocol

Chauffeurs adhere to etiquette and protocol guidelines to provide exemplary service and enhance the client experience. They observe traffic laws and regulations, including speed limits and parking restrictions, to maintain compliance and safety standards. Chauffeurs demonstrate courteous behavior, including opening doors for clients, assisting with seating arrangements, and accommodating special requests to exceed client expectations and foster positive relationships.

Technology Integration

Advancements in technology enhance the efficiency and service delivery of chauffeurs, enabling seamless communication, navigation, and client management. Chauffeurs utilize mobile applications for scheduling appointments, managing client preferences, and coordinating travel logistics with dispatch or concierge services. Integrated communication systems facilitate real-time updates and client notifications, ensuring clear and timely communication throughout the journey.

Regulatory Compliance

Chauffeurs adhere to regulatory requirements governing transportation services, including licensing, insurance coverage, and background checks to ensure eligibility and professionalism. They maintain accurate records of travel activities, including mileage logs, client receipts, and service agreements, to document compliance with industry standards and legal obligations. Chauffeurs participate in ongoing training and professional development programs to stay informed about regulatory changes and industry best practices.

Career Development Opportunities

A career as a chauffeur offers opportunities for professional growth and advancement within the hospitality, transportation, and private service industries. Experienced chauffeurs may pursue leadership roles in fleet management, client relations, or concierge services, overseeing operations and enhancing service quality. Professional development programs and certifications in luxury service, client management, and executive transport prepare chauffeurs for career progression and specialized assignments.

Personal Perspectives
Personal narratives from chauffeurs provide insights into the rewards, challenges, and unique experiences of working in private transportation services. They share firsthand accounts of memorable interactions with clients, navigating diverse travel destinations, and delivering exceptional service under varying conditions. Chauffeurs reflect on the pride and satisfaction of exceeding client expectations, building lasting relationships, and contributing to memorable travel experiences.

Chapter 7. Construction Vehicles

Construction vehicle operators play a vital role in the construction industry, operating heavy machinery and equipment to support diverse construction projects. Through their expertise, dedication to safety, and commitment to quality and efficiency, operators contribute to the success and sustainability of construction operations, infrastructure development, and community enhancement efforts worldwide.

Roles and Responsibilities
Construction vehicle operators play a critical role in the construction industry, operating heavy machinery and equipment essential for various construction projects. Their primary responsibility is to safely and efficiently maneuver construction vehicles, such as excavators, bulldozers, cranes, and dump trucks, to perform tasks such as earthmoving, excavation, material handling, and site preparation. Operators adhere to safety protocols, construction plans, and project specifications to support the timely completion of construction projects while ensuring worksite safety.

Types of Construction Vehicles
Construction vehicles encompass a diverse range of equipment tailored to specific construction tasks and site conditions. Common types of construction vehicles include:

Excavators: Used for digging trenches, foundations, and landscaping projects.

Bulldozers: Crucially employed in construction for earthmoving, grading terrain, and pushing heavy materials with efficiency and power.

Cranes: Essential for lifting and positioning heavy materials and equipment.

Dump Trucks: Transport materials such as gravel, dirt, and debris within construction sites.

Backhoes: Combined loader and excavator used for digging, lifting, and loading materials.

Graders: Specialized vehicles used extensively in construction for leveling and grading surfaces, particularly for roads, foundations, and other large-scale projects requiring precise surface preparation.

Concrete mixers: Essential for blending and transporting concrete to construction sites efficiently.

Each type of construction vehicle requires specialized training and certification to operate safely and effectively in accordance with manufacturer guidelines and industry standards.

Safety Protocols and Procedures

Safety is paramount in construction vehicle operations, with operators trained in safety protocols and procedures to prevent accidents and ensure worksite safety. Operators conduct pre-operational inspections of construction vehicles to verify mechanical integrity, functionality of safety features, and compliance with operational standards. They adhere to Occupational Safety and Health Administration (OSHA) regulations and industry best practices for equipment operation, personal protective equipment (PPE) use, and hazard mitigation to minimize risks and promote a safe working environment.

Site Preparation and Operation

Construction vehicle operators play a crucial role in site preparation and operation, collaborating with construction teams and site supervisors to execute project plans efficiently. They interpret construction blueprints, layouts, and specifications to determine optimal equipment placement and operational strategies. Operators adjust equipment settings, such as blade heights or digging depths, to meet project requirements and ensure accurate execution of construction tasks, such as excavation, grading, and material handling.

Environmental Considerations

Construction vehicle operators prioritize environmental stewardship by implementing practices to minimize environmental impacts during construction activities. They adhere to environmental regulations and permit requirements governing soil erosion, water runoff, and air quality to protect natural resources and wildlife habitats. Operators employ dust suppression techniques, such as watering or covering materials, to mitigate airborne particles and maintain air quality standards on construction sites.

Maintenance and Equipment Care

Maintenance and care of construction vehicles are essential for ensuring equipment reliability, longevity, and operational efficiency. Operators perform routine maintenance tasks, including fluid checks, lubrication, and filter replacements, to prevent mechanical breakdowns and optimize equipment performance. They inspect equipment components, such as hydraulic systems, tracks or tires, and electrical systems, to identify potential issues and schedule repairs with qualified technicians or service providers promptly.

Technological Advancements

Technological advancements enhance the capabilities and efficiency of construction vehicles, improving productivity and operational performance on construction sites. Operators utilize advanced features, such as GPS navigation systems, telematics, and remote monitoring technologies, to optimize equipment utilization, track performance metrics, and enhance operational planning. Integrated sensors and diagnostic tools provide real-time data on equipment health, fuel consumption, and operational parameters to support proactive maintenance and decision-making.

Training and Certification
Construction vehicle operators undergo specialized training and certification programs to acquire the skills and knowledge necessary for safe and effective equipment operation. Training programs cover equipment operation techniques, safety protocols, regulatory compliance, and emergency procedures to prepare operators for diverse construction environments and operational challenges. Certification requirements vary by jurisdiction and equipment type, with operators maintaining ongoing training and professional development to stay abreast of industry advancements and regulatory changes.

Career Opportunities
A career as a construction vehicle operator offers opportunities for professional growth and advancement within the construction industry. Experienced operators may pursue specialized roles in equipment maintenance, site supervision, project management, or equipment sales and training. Professional development programs and certifications in equipment operation, safety management, and construction technology enable operators to expand their skills and expertise, enhancing career prospects and contributing to industry innovation and development.

Community Impact

Construction vehicle operators contribute to community development and infrastructure improvement by supporting construction projects that enhance transportation networks, public facilities, and residential or commercial developments. They collaborate with construction teams, engineers, and stakeholders to deliver projects that meet quality standards, safety requirements, and environmental considerations. Operators engage with local communities to promote awareness of construction activities, mitigate impacts, and foster positive relationships through transparent communication and community engagement initiatives.

Personal Perspectives

Personal narratives from construction vehicle operators provide insights into the challenges, rewards, and experiences of working in construction equipment operations. Operators share firsthand accounts of overcoming operational challenges, adapting to evolving technologies, and contributing to the successful completion of construction projects. They reflect on the satisfaction of operating specialized equipment, collaborating with skilled professionals, and witnessing tangible outcomes that improve communities and infrastructure.

Chapter 8. Courier and Messenger Drivers

Courier and messenger drivers play a vital role in the logistics and delivery industry, providing essential transportation services and fostering customer satisfaction through efficient, reliable, and personalized delivery experiences. Through their dedication, professionalism, and commitment to service excellence, drivers contribute to the success and efficiency of supply chain operations, supporting commerce and connectivity in local and global economies.

Roles and Responsibilities
Courier and messenger drivers are integral to the logistics and delivery industry, responsible for transporting packages, documents, and goods between locations efficiently and securely. Their primary role is to ensure timely delivery of items while maintaining high standards of customer service and professionalism. Courier drivers manage delivery schedules, route planning, and customer interactions to meet delivery deadlines and exceed client expectations.

Delivery Operations
The daily operations of courier and messenger drivers revolve around managing delivery assignments, coordinating with dispatchers or logistics coordinators, and navigating delivery routes effectively. Drivers prioritize delivery schedules based on urgency and customer preferences, utilizing GPS navigation systems and real-time traffic updates to optimize route efficiency and minimize delivery times. They handle parcels with care, ensuring proper handling, loading, and unloading to prevent damage or loss during transit.

Customer Service Excellence

Courier and messenger drivers excel at customer service, providing personalized delivery experiences and fostering positive relationships with clients. They greet customers courteously, confirm delivery details, and obtain signatures or proof of delivery to ensure accountability and client satisfaction. Drivers communicate proactively with customers, providing updates on delivery status, anticipated arrival times, and resolving inquiries or concerns promptly to enhance the overall customer experience.

Vehicle Maintenance and Safety

Maintaining vehicle safety and reliability is essential for courier and messenger drivers to ensure operational efficiency and adherence to delivery schedules. Drivers conduct pre-trip inspections of vehicles, checking tire pressure, fluid levels, brakes, and safety equipment to confirm vehicle readiness and compliance with safety standards. They report any mechanical issues or maintenance needs promptly to fleet managers or service providers to minimize downtime and ensure safe transportation of goods.

Adaptability and Time Management

Courier and messenger drivers demonstrate adaptability and effective time management skills to respond to changing delivery demands and unforeseen circumstances. They prioritize deliveries based on urgency, traffic conditions, and customer requirements, adjusting routes or schedules as needed to meet delivery commitments. Drivers remain flexible and resourceful, navigating through diverse environments, weather conditions, and logistical challenges while maintaining delivery accuracy and efficiency.

Technology Integration

Technological advancements enhance the efficiency and effectiveness of courier and messenger delivery services, enabling drivers to streamline operations and improve service quality.

Drivers utilize mobile applications or handheld devices for route optimization, real-time tracking of deliveries, and electronic proof of delivery (ePOD) capture. Integrated communication systems facilitate instant updates with dispatchers or customers, ensuring clear and accurate information exchange throughout the delivery process.

Regulatory Compliance

Courier and messenger drivers adhere to regulatory requirements governing transportation, including driver licensing, vehicle registration, and insurance coverage for commercial operations. They maintain accurate records of delivery activities, including mileage logs, delivery receipts, and customer signatures, to document compliance with industry standards and legal obligations. Drivers undergo training in defensive driving techniques, cargo handling procedures, and customer confidentiality to uphold safety and operational standards.

Environmental Responsibility

Courier and messenger drivers contribute to environmental sustainability by adopting eco-friendly practices and fuel-efficient driving techniques. They optimize delivery routes to minimize fuel consumption and reduce carbon emissions, supporting environmental conservation efforts and sustainable transportation practices. Drivers comply with environmental regulations, waste disposal guidelines, and energy-efficient vehicle maintenance to minimize ecological impact and promote a greener delivery operation.

Career Development Opportunities

A career as a courier or messenger driver offers opportunities for professional growth and advancement within the logistics and transportation industry. Experienced drivers may pursue roles in logistics management, fleet operations, or customer service management, overseeing delivery operations and enhancing service excellence. Professional development programs and certifications in logistics management, supply chain operations, and courier services equip drivers with skills and knowledge for career progression and leadership roles.

Community Engagement

Courier and messenger drivers engage with local communities by providing essential delivery services, supporting businesses, and facilitating economic growth. They collaborate with businesses, retailers, and e-commerce platforms to fulfill delivery orders, promote local commerce, and enhance consumer access to goods and services. Drivers participate in community events, charitable initiatives, and outreach programs to strengthen community relationships, support social causes, and contribute positively to local economies.

Personal Perspectives

Drivers share stories of navigating diverse delivery assignments, overcoming logistical hurdles, and building rapport with customers and colleagues. They reflect on the satisfaction of meeting delivery deadlines, exceeding customer expectations, and contributing to the seamless flow of goods and information in today's interconnected world.

Chapter 9. Delivery Drivers

Delivery drivers play a vital role in the logistics and transportation industries, providing essential delivery services, fostering customer satisfaction, and supporting operational efficiency across various sectors. Through their dedication, professionalism, and commitment to service excellence, delivery drivers contribute to the success of businesses, enhance consumer access to goods and services, and facilitate economic growth and community development worldwide.

Roles and Responsibilities
Delivery drivers are integral to the logistics and transportation sectors, responsible for transporting goods, merchandise, and packages to customers or businesses efficiently and safely. Their primary role involves loading, transporting, and unloading deliveries while adhering to delivery schedules, customer requirements, and safety protocols. Delivery drivers play a crucial role in ensuring timely and accurate delivery of goods, maintaining customer satisfaction, and supporting operational efficiency in various industries.

Types of Delivery Drivers
Delivery drivers encompass a diverse range of roles and specialties tailored to specific industries and delivery requirements. Common types of delivery drivers include:

Parcel Delivery Drivers: Responsible for delivering small packages and parcels to residential or commercial addresses.

Food Delivery Drivers: Deliver food orders from restaurants, cafes, or food delivery platforms to customers' locations.

Retail Delivery Drivers: Transport merchandise and goods from distribution centers or warehouses to retail stores or businesses.

Courier Drivers: Provide express delivery services for documents, packages, or time-sensitive deliveries across local or regional areas.

Freight Delivery Drivers: Operate heavy-duty vehicles to transport large shipments, freight, or bulk goods over long distances.

Each type of delivery driver requires specialized training, vehicle operation skills, and knowledge of industry-specific regulations to ensure efficient and secure delivery services.

Customer Service Excellence

Delivery drivers prioritize customer service excellence by providing courteous and professional interactions with recipients or customers. They greet customers or recipients upon delivery, confirm package contents, obtain signatures or proof of delivery, and address customer inquiries or concerns promptly. Delivery drivers ensure the safe handling and proper placement of deliveries, adhering to customer preferences and delivery instructions to enhance the overall customer experience.

Route Planning and Navigation

Efficient route planning and navigation skills are essential for delivery drivers to optimize delivery routes, minimize travel time, and meet delivery deadlines. They utilize GPS navigation systems, digital maps, or route optimization software to plan efficient delivery routes, avoid traffic congestion, and identify alternative routes as needed. Delivery drivers adapt to changing traffic conditions, road closures, or weather hazards while maintaining delivery schedule adherence and ensuring timely deliveries.

Vehicle Maintenance and Safety

Maintaining vehicle safety and operational readiness is critical for delivery drivers to ensure reliable and secure transportation of goods. Drivers perform routine inspections of delivery vehicles, checking tire pressure, fluid levels, brakes, and safety equipment to ensure compliance with safety standards and manufacturer specifications. They report any mechanical issues or maintenance needs promptly to fleet managers or service providers to minimize downtime and uphold vehicle reliability during delivery operations.

Environmental Responsibility

Delivery drivers contribute to environmental sustainability by adopting eco-friendly practices and fuel-efficient driving techniques. They optimize delivery routes to minimize fuel consumption, reduce carbon emissions, and support environmental conservation efforts. Drivers adhere to environmental regulations, waste management guidelines, and energy-efficient vehicle maintenance practices to minimize ecological impact and promote sustainable delivery operations within communities and urban areas.

Technology Integration

Advancements in technology enhance the efficiency and effectiveness of delivery operations, enabling drivers to streamline delivery processes and improve service reliability. Delivery drivers utilize mobile applications or handheld devices for real-time tracking of deliveries, electronic proof of delivery (ePOD) capture, and communication with dispatchers or customers. Integrated communication systems facilitate instant updates on delivery status, address verification, and customer notifications to ensure transparency and operational efficiency throughout the delivery process.

Regulatory Compliance

Delivery drivers adhere to regulatory requirements governing transportation services, including driver licensing, vehicle registration, insurance coverage, and adherence to traffic laws and safety regulations. They maintain accurate records of delivery activities, including mileage logs, delivery receipts, and customer signatures, to document compliance with industry standards and legal obligations. Drivers participate in ongoing training and professional development programs to stay informed about regulatory changes, enhance driving skills, and maintain safety standards.

Career Development Opportunities
A career as a delivery driver offers opportunities for professional growth and advancement within the logistics, transportation, and delivery sectors. Experienced drivers may pursue specialized roles in route planning, fleet management, customer service management, or logistics operations. Professional development programs and certifications in logistics management, supply chain operations, and delivery services equip drivers with skills and expertise for career progression and leadership roles within the industry.

Community Engagement
Delivery drivers contribute to community engagement by providing essential delivery services that support local businesses, residential communities, and economic activities. They collaborate with businesses, retailers, and e-commerce platforms to fulfill delivery orders, promote consumer access to goods and services, and stimulate local commerce. Drivers engage with local communities through participation in charitable initiatives, community events, and outreach programs to enhance community relationships, support social causes, and contribute positively to the local economy.

Personal Perspectives

Delivery drivers share stories of navigating diverse delivery assignments, overcoming logistical obstacles, and building rapport with customers and colleagues. They reflect on the satisfaction of meeting delivery deadlines, exceeding customer expectations, and contributing to the efficient movement of goods and services in today's interconnected global economy.

Chapter 10. Driving School Instructors

Driving school instructors play a vital role in preparing new drivers for safe and responsible driving practices through comprehensive driver education programs. Through their expertise, dedication to safety, and commitment to student success, instructors contribute to the cultivation of competent drivers who uphold traffic laws, practice defensive driving techniques, and promote road safety within their communities.

Roles and Responsibilities
Driving school instructors play a pivotal role in preparing new drivers for safe and responsible driving practices on the road. Their primary responsibility is to provide comprehensive driving instruction and education to learners, ensuring they develop essential driving skills, knowledge of traffic laws, and confidence behind the wheel. Instructors create structured learning environments, deliver engaging lessons, and assess student progress to facilitate the successful completion of driver education programs and licensing requirements.

Curriculum Development
Driving school instructors develop and tailor instructional curricula to meet the needs and learning objectives of diverse student demographics. They design lesson plans, teaching materials, and practical driving exercises that align with state or provincial driver education standards and regulatory requirements. Instructors integrate theoretical knowledge, defensive driving techniques, and hands-on driving experiences to equip students with the skills and competence needed to navigate various road conditions and traffic scenarios safely.

Instructor Certification and Training

Becoming a certified driving school instructor requires completing specialized training programs and obtaining instructor certification from recognized driver education authorities or licensing agencies. Instructors undergo rigorous training in teaching methodologies, instructional techniques, traffic safety regulations, and vehicle operation principles to deliver effective driver education programs. Certification programs include practical assessments, classroom instruction, and on-road evaluations to ensure instructors possess the expertise and qualifications to teach aspiring drivers.

Student Assessment and Progress Evaluation

Driving school instructors assess student learning and driving proficiency through systematic evaluations, progress assessments, and performance reviews. They conduct written examinations, practical driving tests, and simulated driving scenarios to evaluate student comprehension, skill development, and adherence to traffic laws and safety protocols. Instructors provide constructive feedback, guidance, and coaching to help students address areas for improvement and achieve mastery of essential driving competencies required for safe and responsible driving.

Teaching Techniques and Instructional Methods

Instructors employ a variety of teaching techniques and instructional methods to accommodate diverse learning styles and student abilities. They use interactive classroom discussions, multimedia presentations, and visual aids to enhance their theoretical understanding of traffic laws, road signs, and driving principles. In practical driving sessions, instructors demonstrate driving maneuvers, facilitate hands-on practice sessions, and use dual-control vehicles to ensure safety and control during student driving exercises.

Safety and Risk Management

Safety is paramount in driver education, with instructors emphasizing the importance of defensive driving techniques, hazard awareness, and proactive risk management strategies. They educate students on anticipating potential hazards, reacting to unexpected road conditions, and maintaining situational awareness to prevent accidents and promote road safety. Instructors enforce strict adherence to safety protocols, vehicle operation guidelines, and traffic laws to cultivate responsible driving behaviors and minimize the risk of collisions or traffic violations.

Professional Ethics and Conduct

Driving school instructors uphold professional ethics, integrity, and standards of conduct in their interactions with students, parents, and licensing authorities. They maintain the confidentiality of student records, respect diverse cultural backgrounds, and provide unbiased and impartial instruction to all learners. Instructors demonstrate patience, empathy, and professionalism while addressing student concerns, resolving conflicts, and fostering a positive learning environment conducive to driver skill development and confidence building.

Technology Integration in Driver Education

Advancements in technology enhance the effectiveness and efficiency of driver education programs, enabling instructors to incorporate interactive simulations, virtual reality (VR) training modules, and computer-based driving simulations into curriculum delivery. Instructors utilize digital learning platforms, online resources, and educational apps to supplement traditional classroom instruction and provide students with interactive learning experiences. Technology integration supports personalized learning, real-time feedback, and enhanced student engagement in driver education courses.

Career Development and Continuing Education

A career as a driving school instructor offers opportunities for professional growth and advancement within the field of driver education. Instructors may pursue specialized certifications, advanced training programs, or continuing education courses in traffic safety, defensive driving techniques, and instructional methodologies. Professional development enhances instructors' teaching skills, expands their knowledge base, and prepares them for leadership roles, curriculum development, or educational administration in driver education programs.

Community Engagement and Impact

Driving school instructors contribute to community safety and traffic education initiatives by equipping new drivers with essential skills, knowledge, and responsible driving behaviors. They collaborate with schools, community organizations, and traffic safety advocates to promote awareness of traffic laws, reduce traffic accidents, and improve road safety within local communities. Instructors engage with parents, stakeholders, and policymakers to advocate for effective driver education programs, legislative reforms, and initiatives that support safe driving practices and accident prevention strategies.

Personal Perspectives

Driving school instructors share stories of mentoring aspiring drivers, witnessing student progress, and celebrating milestones such as obtaining driver's licenses. They reflect on the fulfillment of empowering individuals with life-changing driving skills, promoting road safety, and contributing to the development of competent and responsible drivers who enhance transportation safety and mobility in their communities.

Chapter 11. Emergency Vehicle Drivers

Emergency vehicle drivers play a vital role in emergency medical services, providing rapid response, patient care, and transportation to individuals in medical crises. Through their dedication, specialized training, and commitment to patient safety, drivers contribute to the effectiveness of emergency response systems, promote public health and safety, and ensure timely access to lifesaving medical care within communities and urban areas.

Roles and Responsibilities
Emergency vehicle drivers are essential personnel responsible for transporting medical personnel, equipment, and patients swiftly and safely to emergency scenes or healthcare facilities. Their primary role involves operating specialized emergency vehicles, such as ambulances or paramedic units, while prioritizing patient care, safety, and adherence to traffic laws. Emergency drivers navigate through traffic, respond to emergency calls, and provide timely medical assistance to patients in critical situations, demonstrating proficiency in emergency vehicle operations and medical transport protocols.

Emergency Response Protocols
Emergency vehicle drivers adhere to established emergency response protocols and procedures to ensure a rapid and effective response to medical emergencies. They collaborate with emergency medical services (EMS) teams, dispatchers, and healthcare professionals to coordinate emergency response efforts, prioritize patient transport based on medical urgency, and navigate optimal routes to emergency scenes or healthcare facilities. Drivers maintain clear communication with dispatchers,

update response status, and adjust driving tactics to ensure safe and efficient emergency vehicle operations.

Patient Care and Transport
Emergency vehicle drivers prioritize patient care and safety during medical transport, providing compassionate support and medical assistance to patients in transit. They assess patient conditions, administer basic medical treatments or life-saving interventions as needed, and monitor vital signs to stabilize patients' medical status during transport. Drivers ensure secure patient immobilization, maintain infection control measures, and communicate patient information to receiving medical personnel to facilitate seamless transfer and continuity of care.

Vehicle Operations and Safety
Operating emergency vehicles requires specialized training in vehicle handling, defensive driving techniques, and emergency response operations. Drivers undergo rigorous training and certification in emergency vehicle operations (EVO), including vehicle maneuvering, emergency braking, and navigating through traffic safely under emergency conditions. They conduct pre-trip inspections, ensure equipment readiness, and adhere to vehicle maintenance schedules to uphold operational readiness and compliance with safety standards during emergency responses.

Navigation and Route Planning
Emergency vehicle drivers utilize advanced navigation systems, GPS technologies, and digital mapping tools to plan optimal routes, avoid traffic congestion, and minimize response times to emergency incidents. They maintain situational awareness of road conditions, weather hazards, and potential obstacles to navigate efficiently through urban or rural environments. Drivers adapt to changing traffic patterns, road closures, or adverse weather conditions while maintaining vigilance and responsiveness to ensure timely arrival at emergency scenes or healthcare facilities.

Critical Incident Management
Emergency vehicle drivers manage critical incidents and high-stress situations with composure, professionalism, and effective decision-making skills. They assess emergency scenes for safety hazards, collaborate with law enforcement or fire department personnel, and provide logistical support to emergency response teams as needed. Drivers prioritize scene safety, coordinate patient extrication or rescue operations, and facilitate efficient transport of multiple patients or casualties during mass casualty incidents (MCI) or natural disasters.

Communication and Coordination
Effective communication is crucial for emergency vehicle drivers to coordinate with dispatchers, healthcare professionals, and public safety agencies during emergency responses. They maintain clear radio communication, relay critical incident updates, and request additional resources or medical support as necessary. Drivers collaborate with EMS teams, fire departments, and law enforcement agencies to coordinate multi-agency responses, establish incident command structures, and ensure cohesive teamwork in emergency situations.

Regulatory Compliance and Training
Emergency vehicle drivers adhere to regulatory requirements, licensing standards, and certification protocols governing emergency vehicle operations and medical transport services. They maintain valid driver licenses, obtain specialized endorsements for emergency vehicle operation, and participate in ongoing training programs to enhance skills in emergency response, patient care techniques, and compliance with healthcare regulations. Drivers undergo periodic recertification, competency assessments, and continuing education to stay current with industry standards and best practices.

Community Engagement and Public Outreach

Emergency vehicle drivers engage with the community through public education initiatives, safety demonstrations, and outreach programs to promote emergency preparedness and injury prevention strategies. They participate in community events, health fairs, and school presentations to educate residents on the importance of emergency medical services, safe driving practices, and bystander response to medical emergencies. Drivers collaborate with local organizations, advocacy groups, and public health agencies to enhance community awareness, support public health initiatives, and strengthen community resilience.

Personal Perspectives
Emergency vehicle drivers provide firsthand insights into the challenges, rewards, and experiences of serving as frontline responders in emergency medical services. They share stories of lifesaving interventions, teamwork under pressure, and moments of profound impact while providing critical care and transportation to patients in need. They reflect on the privilege of serving their communities, making a difference in emergency situations, and upholding the commitment to excellence in emergency medical transport and patient care.

Chapter 12. Forklift Operators

Forklift operators play a crucial role in industrial material handling operations, supporting warehouse logistics, inventory management, and supply chain efficiency. Through their expertise, adherence to safety protocols, and commitment to operational excellence, forklift operators contribute to workplace safety, productivity, and the seamless movement of materials within warehouses, distribution centers, and manufacturing facilities.

Roles and Responsibilities

Forklift operators are skilled professionals responsible for operating industrial trucks equipped with forks to lift, move, stack, and organize materials within warehouses, distribution centers, or construction sites. Their primary role involves safely maneuvering forklifts to transport goods, pallets, or heavy equipment, following strict safety protocols, and adhering to operational guidelines. Forklift operators play a critical role in maintaining inventory accuracy, optimizing storage space, and supporting efficient material handling operations in diverse industrial settings.

Safety and Equipment Operation

Operating forklifts requires comprehensive training in equipment operation, safety procedures, and load handling techniques to ensure workplace safety and minimize the risk of accidents or injuries. Forklift operators conduct pre-operational inspections of forklifts, checking controls, brakes, hydraulics, and safety features to ensure equipment readiness and compliance with safety standards. They use personal protective equipment (PPE), such as helmets, gloves, and safety vests, and adhere to workplace safety regulations to mitigate hazards and promote a safe working environment.

Material Handling and Inventory Management

Forklift operators specialize in loading and unloading materials, pallets, or products from trucks, storage racks, or production areas using forklift attachments, such as forks or clamps. They transport materials to designated locations, stack goods in storage areas, and arrange inventory according to organizational requirements or inventory management systems. Operators maintain inventory accuracy, record material movements, and update inventory records to facilitate efficient stock replenishment, order fulfillment, and supply chain operations.

Warehouse Operations and Logistics Support

Forklift operators contribute to warehouse operations by supporting logistics activities, order processing, and fulfillment operations within distribution centers or manufacturing facilities. They collaborate with warehouse supervisors, logistics coordinators, and inventory control teams to prioritize workload, expedite material flow, and meet production schedules. Operators assist in receiving shipments, verifying product quantities, and coordinating with shipping departments to prepare outgoing orders for timely delivery to customers or distribution points.

Equipment Maintenance and Performance

Maintaining forklift performance and operational efficiency is essential for forklift operators to ensure reliable equipment operation and productivity in material handling operations. Operators conduct routine maintenance checks, lubricate components, and perform minor repairs or adjustments to forklifts to prevent equipment breakdowns and prolong service life. They report mechanical issues or safety concerns to maintenance technicians or supervisors promptly and participate in equipment training programs to enhance forklift operation skills and troubleshooting abilities.

Load Handling and Safety Practices

Forklift operators employ safe load handling practices to secure and transport loads of varying sizes, weights, or shapes without compromising workplace safety or stability. They utilize load handling attachments, such as pallet forks, drum clamps, or carton clamps, to lift, position, and maneuver materials effectively. Operators assess load capacities, distribute weights evenly, and adjust forklift settings to maintain balance, stability, and control during load handling operations. They adhere to safe stacking procedures, aisle navigation guidelines, and traffic management protocols to prevent accidents and maintain operational efficiency.

Regulatory Compliance and Certification
Forklift operators comply with regulatory requirements and industry standards governing forklift operation, workplace safety, and occupational health. They obtain forklift operator certification through accredited training programs, practical assessments, and written examinations to demonstrate proficiency in forklift operation skills, safety awareness, and regulatory compliance. Operators renew certifications periodically, undergo refresher training, and stay informed about legislative updates or safety regulations to uphold workplace safety standards and promote safe forklift operation practices.

Environmental Awareness and Sustainability
Forklift operators promote environmental awareness and sustainability by adopting eco-friendly practices, energy-efficient equipment operation techniques, and waste management initiatives within warehouse or industrial environments. They minimize fuel consumption, reduce carbon emissions, and optimize energy usage by implementing forklift idle reduction strategies, energy-saving technologies, and recycling programs. Operators participate in environmental stewardship programs, support sustainability initiatives, and collaborate with environmental health and safety (EHS) teams to promote eco-

conscious practices and minimize environmental impact in material handling operations.

Career Development Opportunities
A career as a forklift operator offers opportunities for professional growth, skill development, and advancement within the logistics, warehousing, and supply chain sectors. Operators may pursue advanced training in specialized forklift operations, equipment maintenance, or warehouse management to expand their skills and qualifications. Professional development programs, certifications in logistics management, or leadership training equip operators with the expertise to pursue supervisory roles, team leadership positions, or career advancement opportunities in warehouse operations or material handling management.

Personal Perspectives
Forklift operators share stories of navigating warehouse environments, overcoming logistical obstacles, and ensuring timely material delivery to support production deadlines or customer demands. They reflect on the satisfaction of contributing to efficient supply chain operations, maintaining workplace safety, and mastering the art of forklift operation to enhance productivity and organizational success.

Chapter 13. Garbage Truck Drivers

Garbage truck drivers play a vital role in municipal waste management, sanitation services, and environmental stewardship by ensuring efficient waste collection, promoting recycling efforts, and maintaining community cleanliness. Through their dedication, professionalism, and commitment to service excellence, drivers contribute to sustainable waste practices, public health protection, and community well-being by delivering reliable waste management solutions and fostering environmental responsibility within urban and suburban areas.

Roles and Responsibilities
Garbage truck drivers are essential frontline workers responsible for collecting, transporting, and disposing of municipal or commercial waste from residential neighborhoods, businesses, and public areas. Their primary role involves operating specialized garbage trucks, such as rear-loaders or front-loaders, to collect waste containers, bins, or dumpsters along designated routes. Garbage truck drivers play a critical role in maintaining sanitation standards, promoting public health, and ensuring efficient waste management practices within communities.

Waste Collection and Route Management
Garbage truck drivers manage waste collection routes, schedules, and pickup locations to ensure the timely and systematic removal of solid waste materials. They navigate through residential neighborhoods, commercial districts, or industrial areas to collect waste containers, empty dumpsters, and load garbage into truck compartments using hydraulic lift mechanisms or automated loading systems. Drivers optimize route efficiency, adhere to collection guidelines, and adjust schedules based on seasonal

demands or special events to meet waste disposal needs effectively.

Vehicle Operation and Safety

Operating garbage trucks requires specialized training in vehicle operation, maneuvering techniques, and safety procedures to minimize accidents or hazards during waste collection activities. Drivers conduct pre-trip inspections and check vehicle controls, hydraulics, and safety features to ensure equipment readiness and compliance with safety regulations. They utilize personal protective equipment (PPE), such as gloves, reflective vests, and safety goggles, and follow established protocols for waste handling, lifting heavy loads, and securing garbage containers to prevent spills or injuries.

Recycling and Waste Diversion

Garbage truck drivers support recycling and waste diversion initiatives by identifying and separating recyclable materials from general waste during collection routes. They implement recycling programs, educate residents or businesses on proper waste segregation practices, and promote environmental sustainability by diverting recyclable materials from landfills. Drivers collaborate with recycling centers, waste management facilities, and environmental agencies to facilitate recycling efforts, reduce landfill waste, and support community recycling goals.

Public Relations and Customer Service

Garbage truck drivers interact with residents, business owners, and community members during waste collection activities, demonstrating professionalism, courtesy, and responsiveness to customer inquiries or service requests. They address customer concerns, provide assistance with bulky item pickups or special waste disposal requests, and ensure positive public relations through respectful communication and effective problem-solving. Drivers foster community engagement, promote waste reduction behaviors, and contribute to community cleanliness and environmental stewardship initiatives.

Environmental Compliance and Regulatory Standards

Garbage truck drivers comply with environmental regulations, waste disposal laws, and regulatory standards governing solid waste management and sanitation practices. They adhere to local, state, or federal guidelines for waste collection, transportation, and disposal procedures to protect environmental quality, prevent pollution, and mitigate potential health risks associated with improper waste handling. Drivers maintain records of waste collection activities, report hazardous materials or illegal dumping incidents, and participate in environmental audits or compliance inspections to uphold regulatory compliance and environmental sustainability.

Team Collaboration and Operational Efficiency

Garbage truck drivers collaborate with waste management teams, route supervisors, and maintenance crews to optimize operational efficiency, streamline waste collection processes, and address operational challenges in real-time. They communicate effectively with dispatchers, coordinate vehicle maintenance schedules, and assist in fleet management activities to ensure reliable vehicle performance and uninterrupted waste collection services. Drivers contribute to team success, support fellow crew members during peak workload periods, and promote teamwork in achieving departmental goals and service excellence.

Health and Safety Practices

Maintaining health and safety is paramount for garbage truck drivers, who follow strict safety protocols, ergonomic practices, and risk management strategies to prevent work-related injuries or accidents. They undergo training in manual handling techniques, lifting procedures, and ergonomic principles to minimize physical strain, fatigue, and musculoskeletal injuries during waste collection activities. Drivers prioritize personal safety, vehicle maintenance, and adherence to safety guidelines to create a safe working environment and protect themselves and their colleagues from occupational hazards.

Technological Integration and Innovation

Advancements in waste management technologies enhance operational efficiency and productivity for garbage truck drivers. They utilize onboard computer systems, GPS tracking devices, and route optimization software to plan efficient collection routes, monitor vehicle performance, and track waste collection progress in real-time. Drivers leverage digital platforms, mobile applications, and telematics solutions to report service issues, communicate with dispatchers, and facilitate data-driven decision-making for improved service delivery and customer satisfaction.

Career Development and Training

A career as a garbage truck driver offers opportunities for professional growth, skill development, and advancement within the waste management industry. Drivers may pursue specialized training in hazardous materials handling, waste management technologies, or leadership skills to enhance career opportunities and qualifications. Professional development programs, industry certifications, and continuing education courses equip drivers with the knowledge and expertise to pursue supervisory roles, fleet management positions, or career advancement opportunities in waste management operations.

Personal Perspectives

Garbage truck drivers provide firsthand insights about waste management and sanitation services. Drivers share stories of navigating residential neighborhoods, handling diverse waste materials, and fostering community relationships through reliable waste collection services. They reflect on the pride of contributing to environmental sustainability, promoting public health, and ensuring clean, livable communities through responsible waste management practices.

Chapter 14. Heavy Equipment Operators

Heavy equipment operators play a vital role in construction site operations, earthmoving projects, and infrastructure development by operating advanced machinery, ensuring site safety, and supporting efficient project execution. Through their expertise, commitment to safety, and dedication to construction excellence, operators contribute to building resilient infrastructure, promoting sustainable development, and advancing the construction industry's capacity to meet infrastructure demands and community needs.

Roles and Responsibilities

Heavy equipment operators are skilled professionals responsible for operating large machinery and construction equipment to perform various tasks on construction sites, infrastructure projects, or industrial facilities. Their primary role involves maneuvering and controlling equipment such as bulldozers, excavators, cranes, and loaders to excavate earth, move materials, and facilitate construction activities. Heavy equipment operators play a critical role in site preparation, earthmoving operations, and ensuring efficient project execution in the construction and civil engineering sectors.

Equipment Operation and Maintenance

Operating heavy equipment requires specialized training in equipment operation, safety protocols, and maintenance procedures to ensure equipment reliability and performance on construction sites. Operators conduct pre-operational inspections, check hydraulic systems, engine functions, and safety features to maintain equipment readiness and compliance with safety regulations. They utilize advanced controls, attachments, and technology integrated into machinery to enhance operational efficiency, productivity, and precision in handling materials, excavating terrain, or lifting heavy loads.

Site Preparation and Earthmoving

Heavy equipment operators perform site preparation tasks, including grading, leveling, and excavating land to prepare construction sites for building foundations, roadways, or utility installations. They use bulldozers, graders, and excavators to clear vegetation, remove debris, and create level surfaces for construction activities. Operators manipulate equipment controls, adjust blade angles or bucket positions, and coordinate with construction crews to execute grading plans, soil compaction, and earthmoving operations according to project specifications and engineering drawings.

Material Handling and Transport

Heavy equipment operators handle and transport construction materials, aggregates, or heavy components using machinery equipped with lifting attachments or material handling devices. They load, unload, and position materials such as concrete pipes, steel beams, or prefabricated structures within construction sites or industrial yards. Operators secure loads, maintain load stability, and adhere to lifting capacity limits to ensure safe material handling operations, prevent equipment damage, and promote workplace safety during transportation and logistics activities.

Construction Projects and Operations

Heavy equipment operators support construction projects by operating specialized machinery for excavation, trenching, and foundation work on building sites, infrastructure projects, or civil engineering developments. They collaborate with construction managers, project engineers, and site supervisors to execute construction plans, meet project deadlines, and achieve operational milestones. Operators adapt to changing site conditions, environmental factors, and project requirements while adhering to safety regulations, quality standards, and operational guidelines to optimize construction project outcomes.

Safety and Risk Management

Maintaining safety is paramount for heavy equipment operators who follow stringent safety protocols, risk assessment procedures, and hazard mitigation strategies to prevent accidents or injuries on construction sites. Operators undergo training in workplace safety, hazard recognition, and emergency response protocols to promote a safe working environment and minimize occupational risks associated with heavy equipment operation. They utilize personal protective equipment (PPE), such as hard hats, safety glasses, and steel-toe boots, and implement safety measures to protect themselves and coworkers from work-related hazards.

Environmental Compliance and Sustainability

Heavy equipment operators adhere to environmental regulations, sustainability initiatives, and regulatory standards governing construction site operations and land development practices. They implement erosion control measures, minimize soil disturbance, and manage construction waste to mitigate environmental impact and promote sustainable construction practices. Operators support environmental stewardship efforts, participate in resource conservation programs, and adopt green building technologies to enhance environmental sustainability and minimize construction-related impacts on natural ecosystems.

Technological Integration and Innovation

Advancements in construction technology and equipment innovation enhance operational efficiency and productivity for heavy equipment operators. They utilize GPS systems, telematics solutions, and remote monitoring technologies to optimize equipment performance, track machine utilization, and improve operational planning on construction sites. Operators leverage digital platforms, equipment automation, and real-time data analytics to enhance equipment diagnostics, preventive maintenance scheduling, and decision-making processes for effective construction project management and cost control.

Career Development and Training

A career as a heavy equipment operator offers opportunities for professional growth, skill development, and career advancement within the construction and heavy machinery industries. Operators may pursue specialized training in equipment operation, certification programs, or continuing education courses to enhance technical skills, equipment proficiency, and job qualifications. Professional development initiatives, apprenticeship programs, and mentorship opportunities enable operators to advance their careers, pursue supervisory roles, or specialize in specific equipment types or construction disciplines.

Personal Perspectives

Heavy equipment operators provide firsthand insights about operating heavy machinery in construction and civil engineering projects. Operators share stories of overcoming operational challenges, achieving project milestones, and contributing to infrastructure development through skilled equipment operation. They reflect on the satisfaction of shaping landscapes, building foundations, and supporting construction teams to deliver quality workmanship, efficiency, and safety in construction operations.

Chapter 15. Ice Cream Truck Drivers

Ice cream truck drivers play a unique and important role in mobile food service operations, community engagement, and customer satisfaction by delivering delightful ice cream treats, fostering positive experiences, and contributing to local neighborhoods. Through their dedication to customer service, business management skills, and entrepreneurial spirit, ice cream truck drivers create joyful moments, promote community connections, and uphold the tradition of ice cream enjoyment for generations to come.

Roles and Responsibilities

Ice cream truck drivers are mobile vendors responsible for operating ice cream trucks to sell frozen treats, snacks, and beverages in residential neighborhoods, parks, or community events. Their primary role involves driving ice cream trucks to designated locations, attracting customers, and serving a variety of ice cream products to children and families. Ice cream truck drivers play a crucial role in creating enjoyable experiences, promoting customer satisfaction, and generating revenue through mobile food service operations.

Route Planning and Sales Strategy

Ice cream truck drivers plan daily routes, select strategic locations, and schedule stops to maximize sales opportunities and customer engagement. They identify high-traffic areas, popular events, or community gatherings to attract potential customers and increase sales volume. Drivers adjust routes based on weather conditions, seasonal demand, or customer preferences for ice cream flavors, novelty items, or snack options. They promote new products, special promotions, or discounts to enhance sales revenue and build customer loyalty within local communities.

Customer Service and Interaction

Ice cream truck drivers provide friendly customer service, engage with children, families, and community members, and create a welcoming atmosphere for customers to enjoy their ice cream treats. They greet customers, explain menu options, and recommend popular ice cream flavors or specialty items to enhance the customer experience. Drivers handle cash transactions, process payments, and maintain accurate sales records while adhering to food safety regulations, hygiene standards, and quality control measures for food preparation and service.

Inventory Management and Stock Control

Managing inventory and stock levels is essential for ice cream truck drivers to ensure product availability, prevent stock outs, and optimize operational efficiency during daily routes. Drivers monitor inventory levels of ice cream products, frozen treats, snacks, and beverages to replenish supplies, rotate stock, and minimize product wastage. They conduct inventory counts, track product expiration dates, and coordinate with suppliers or distributors to restock inventory and maintain a diverse selection of ice cream products to meet customer preferences and seasonal demands.

Vehicle Maintenance and Safety

Maintaining ice cream trucks in optimal condition is crucial for drivers to ensure reliable vehicle performance, food safety compliance, and customer satisfaction. Drivers conduct routine vehicle inspections, check refrigeration systems, clean food preparation areas, and sanitize serving equipment to uphold food hygiene standards and prevent contamination. They adhere to vehicle maintenance schedules, address mechanical issues promptly, and comply with transportation regulations to ensure the safe operation of ice cream trucks on public roads and during mobile food service operations.

Seasonal Operations and Business Management
Ice cream truck drivers manage seasonal operations, adjust business strategies, and adapt to changing market conditions, weather patterns, and customer preferences throughout the year. They capitalize on peak ice cream consumption periods, such as summer months or community events, to maximize sales revenue and profitability. Drivers implement marketing campaigns, social media promotions, or local advertising initiatives to attract new customers, increase brand visibility, and maintain competitive advantage in the mobile food service industry.

Regulatory Compliance and Licensing
Ice cream truck drivers comply with regulatory requirements, health department regulations, and licensing standards governing mobile food vending operations. They obtain the necessary permits, food handler certifications, and mobile food vendor licenses to operate ice cream trucks legally and ensure food safety compliance. Drivers undergo health inspections, maintain sanitation logs, and follow food handling procedures to mitigate health risks, maintain public trust, and uphold industry standards for mobile food service operations.

Community Engagement and Outreach
Ice cream truck drivers engage with local communities, support charitable events, and participate in community outreach initiatives to foster positive relationships and enhance brand reputation. They sponsor local events, donate ice cream treats, or collaborate with schools, nonprofit organizations, or community centers to promote goodwill, support fundraising efforts, and contribute to community development initiatives. Drivers build rapport with customers, earn trust from families, and create memorable experiences by

delivering quality ice cream products and friendly service to diverse customer demographics.

Entrepreneurial Opportunities and Career Development

A career as an ice cream truck driver offers entrepreneurial opportunities, flexible work schedules, and the potential for business ownership within the mobile food service industry. Drivers may expand their business operations, invest in additional ice cream trucks, or diversify product offerings to increase revenue streams and market reach. Professional development programs, business management courses, or franchise opportunities enable drivers to enhance business acumen, develop leadership skills, and pursue long-term career growth in mobile food service entrepreneurship.

Personal Perspectives

Personal narratives from ice cream truck drivers provide firsthand insights into the joys, challenges, and experiences of operating mobile food service businesses and serving communities through ice cream truck operations. Drivers share stories of connecting with customers, creating memorable moments, and overcoming operational obstacles while spreading joy through delicious ice cream treats. They reflect on the satisfaction of being part of childhood memories, contributing to community celebrations, and building a successful business venture in the mobile food service industry.

Chapter 16. Limousine Drivers

Limousine drivers play a pivotal role in providing premium transportation services, luxury travel experiences, and personalized hospitality for clients seeking comfort, convenience, and style during special occasions or business travel. Through their dedication to service excellence, attention to detail, and commitment to professionalism, limousine drivers elevate the travel experience, cultivate client relationships, and uphold the standard of luxury in the global transportation industry.

Roles and Responsibilities
Limousine drivers, also known as chauffeurs, provide luxury transportation services to clients for various events, special occasions, corporate functions, or leisure travel. Their primary role involves driving limousines, luxury sedans, or executive vehicles to transport passengers safely, comfortably, and stylishly to their destinations. Limousine drivers cater to diverse clientele, including executives, celebrities, wedding parties, and tourists, offering personalized service, discretion, and professionalism to enhance the travel experience.

Client Service and Experience
Limousine drivers prioritize customer service excellence, ensuring a premium travel experience for clients through attentive service, timely arrivals, and courteous behavior. They greet clients with professionalism, assist with luggage handling, and accommodate special requests or preferences during transportation. Drivers maintain a polished appearance, uphold confidentiality, and demonstrate discretion when serving high-profile clients or VIP guests to create a luxurious and comfortable environment throughout the journey.

Event Coordination and Logistics

Limousine drivers coordinate transportation logistics, plan routes, and schedule pickups according to client itineraries, event schedules, or travel arrangements. They collaborate with event planners, concierge services, or personal assistants to coordinate multiple stops, airport transfers, or special event transportation requirements. Drivers navigate traffic conditions, monitor flight schedules, and adjust travel plans in real-time to ensure punctual arrivals, seamless transitions, and efficient transportation services for clients.

Vehicle Maintenance and Presentation

Maintaining limousine vehicles in pristine condition is essential for drivers to ensure passenger safety, vehicle reliability, and aesthetic appeal during luxury transportation services. Drivers conduct pre-trip inspections, check vehicle cleanliness, and perform routine maintenance tasks to ensure the mechanical reliability, interior comfort, and operational readiness of limousine fleets. They adhere to manufacturer guidelines, detailing standards, and cleanliness protocols to present limousines immaculately and create a favorable impression for clients.

Traffic Laws and Safety Protocols

Limousine drivers adhere to traffic laws, regulations, and safety protocols governing commercial passenger transportation to promote safe driving practices and protect passenger well-being. They undergo defensive driving training, traffic management courses, and safety certifications to mitigate risks, avoid accidents, and maintain a clean driving record while operating luxury vehicles on public roads. Drivers prioritize passenger safety, vehicle security, and compliance with transportation regulations to uphold service standards and ensure passenger comfort throughout the journey.

Client Engagement and Communication

Building rapport with clients is essential for limousine drivers to establish trust, understand client preferences, and exceed service expectations during luxury travel experiences. Drivers engage in professional communication, maintain an open dialogue with clients, and anticipate individual needs or preferences to enhance customer satisfaction and loyalty. They provide informative commentary, local knowledge, or concierge services to enrich the travel experience and create memorable moments for clients seeking personalized transportation solutions.

Business Etiquette and Professionalism

Limousine drivers uphold business etiquette, professionalism, and ethical standards when interacting with clients, industry stakeholders, or business partners during luxury transportation services. They demonstrate cultural sensitivity, adapt to diverse client backgrounds, and maintain confidentiality when serving high-profile passengers or corporate executives. Drivers prioritize punctuality, reliability, and integrity in delivering exceptional service, earning client trust, and representing the limousine service brand with distinction in the competitive luxury transportation industry.

Technology Integration and Service Innovation

Advancements in technology and service innovation enhance operational efficiency, client communication, and service delivery for limousine drivers. They utilize GPS navigation systems, mobile apps, and communication tools to optimize route planning, monitor traffic conditions, and provide real-time updates to clients regarding travel schedules or service inquiries. Drivers leverage digital platforms, automated booking systems, and customer feedback mechanisms to streamline reservations, enhance service customization, and maintain service excellence in luxury transportation operations.

Career Development and Industry Trends

A career as a limousine driver offers opportunities for professional growth, skill development, and career advancement within the luxury transportation industry. Drivers may pursue advanced training in hospitality management, customer service excellence, or executive chauffeur certifications to enhance job qualifications and expand career opportunities. Professional development programs, industry networking events, and ongoing education initiatives enable drivers to stay abreast of industry trends, technological advancements, and market demands for luxury transportation services.

Personal Perspectives
Personal narratives from limousine drivers provide firsthand insights about the luxury transportation sector. Drivers share stories of memorable encounters, unique travel experiences, and special moments shared with clients during weddings, corporate events, or private celebrations. They reflect on the pride of delivering exceptional service, exceeding client expectations, and contributing to memorable experiences that define the luxury travel industry.

Chapter 17. Mail Carriers

Mail carriers play a vital role in facilitating mail distribution, supporting communication networks, and providing essential postal services to communities. Through their dedication to service excellence, adherence to postal regulations, and commitment to customer satisfaction, mail carriers uphold the tradition of reliable mail delivery, promote community engagement, and contribute to the efficient operation of postal service networks nationwide.

Roles and Responsibilities
Mail carriers, also known as postal workers or letter carriers, are responsible for delivering mail and parcels to residential or business addresses within designated postal routes. Their primary role involves sorting, organizing, and delivering mail items, packages, or parcels while adhering to postal service regulations, delivery schedules, and customer service standards. Mail carriers play a crucial role in facilitating mail distribution, supporting communication networks, and providing essential postal services to communities across urban, suburban, and rural areas.

Mail Sorting and Distribution
Mail carriers begin their workday at postal facilities, where they receive, sort, and organize incoming mail items, letters, packages, or bulk mail for delivery routes. They use sorting machines, postal codes, or address databases to categorize mail items accurately and prepare delivery routes according to geographic locations or postal zones. Carriers prioritize efficient mail distribution, route optimization, and timely delivery of mail items to ensure reliable postal service, customer satisfaction, and operational efficiency within the postal network.

Delivery Route Management

Managing delivery routes is essential for mail carriers to navigate neighborhoods, apartment complexes, or business districts efficiently and deliver mail items to assigned addresses. They plan daily delivery routes, review route maps or navigation tools, and schedule deliveries based on mail volume, package size, or delivery priorities. Carriers use handheld devices, mobile apps, or GPS navigation systems to track deliveries, update delivery statuses, and record delivery confirmations for accurate mail tracking and customer notification.

Customer Interaction and Service

Mail carriers interact with customers, respond to inquiries, and provide assistance related to postal services, mail delivery schedules, or package tracking information. They deliver mail items to residential mailboxes, apartment buildings, or business premises, ensuring accurate delivery placement, secure handling of packages, and retrieval of undeliverable mail items. Carriers maintain professional communication, address customer concerns, and uphold service standards to enhance customer satisfaction, build trust, and promote positive relationships within the community.

Postal Regulations and Compliance

Adhering to postal regulations, delivery protocols, and safety guidelines is paramount for mail carriers to ensure legal compliance, operational efficiency, and workplace safety during mail delivery operations. They follow postal service policies, delivery instructions, and security procedures to safeguard mail integrity, protect sensitive information, and prevent mail theft or tampering. Carriers undergo training in mail handling practices, hazardous materials awareness, and emergency response protocols to mitigate risks and maintain service reliability in diverse delivery environments.

Environmental Sustainability

Mail carriers support environmental sustainability initiatives, promote paper recycling, and implement eco-friendly practices to reduce carbon footprints and minimize the environmental impact associated with mail delivery operations. They participate in resource conservation programs, optimize delivery routes to reduce fuel consumption, and utilize fuel-efficient vehicles or alternative energy solutions to support sustainable logistics and transportation practices within the postal industry. Carriers advocate for environmental stewardship, adopt green packaging solutions, and embrace technological innovations to enhance operational sustainability and promote environmental responsibility.

Technology Integration and Innovation
Advancements in technology and digital solutions enhance mail delivery efficiency, tracking capabilities, and customer service experiences for mail carriers. They utilize handheld scanners, mobile devices, or electronic signature systems to track delivery progress, capture recipient signatures, and provide real-time updates on mail delivery statuses. Carriers leverage digital platforms, online tracking tools, and automated notifications to inform customers about package deliveries, delivery estimates, or mail service disruptions, enhancing transparency and communication in postal service operations.

Community Engagement and Outreach
Mail carriers engage with local communities, participate in neighborhood events, and support community initiatives to strengthen community bonds, promote postal services, and foster positive relationships with residents. They deliver mail during inclement weather conditions, provide assistance during emergencies, and contribute to community safety by reporting suspicious activities or addressing neighborhood concerns. Carriers build rapport, earn trust, and demonstrate commitment to service excellence by delivering reliable postal services,

supporting community events, and advocating for postal service improvements.

Career Development and Training

A career as a mail carrier provides ample opportunities for career advancement, professional development, and job stability within the postal industry. Carriers may pursue training in postal operations, customer service excellence, or safety protocols to enhance job skills, expand service capabilities, and qualify for promotional opportunities within postal organizations. Professional development programs, leadership training, or continuing education initiatives enable carriers to develop leadership skills, advance career goals, and contribute to operational excellence in postal service delivery.

Personal Perspectives

Personal narratives from mail carriers provide firsthand insights about their experiences of serving as essential workers in the postal industry. Carriers share stories of navigating diverse delivery routes, building relationships with customers, and overcoming logistical challenges while delivering mail in all weather conditions. They reflect on the pride of delivering important communications, greeting familiar faces, and contributing to community connectivity through dependable postal service delivery.

Chapter 18. Metro (Subway) Operators

Metro operators play a pivotal role in urban transit systems by operating subway trains, ensuring passenger safety, and providing essential transportation services to urban communities. Through their dedication to operational excellence, commitment to safety standards, and contribution to public transit efficiency, metro operators uphold the integrity of metro rail networks, promote sustainable urban mobility, and support economic vitality in metropolitan areas worldwide.

Roles and Responsibilities

Metro operators, also known as subway train operators or conductors, are responsible for operating subway trains, ensuring passenger safety, and adhering to transit schedules within urban metro systems. Their primary role involves operating subway trains, monitoring train controls, and managing passenger embarkation and disembarkation at designated stations. Metro operators play a critical role in ensuring efficient subway operations, maintaining commuter safety, and providing reliable public transportation services in densely populated urban areas.

Train Operation and Control

Metro operators operate subway trains and manage train acceleration, braking, and speed control systems to maintain safe and efficient train operations. They follow signal indications, track conditions, and transit schedules to ensure punctual arrivals, departures, and adherence to designated routes within metro rail networks. Operators communicate with transit control centers, dispatchers, or station agents to coordinate train movements, resolve operational issues, and maintain service reliability for commuters traveling on metro lines.

Passenger Safety and Assistance

Ensuring passenger safety is a top priority for metro operators, who oversee passenger boarding, enforce safety protocols, and provide assistance to passengers during emergencies or service disruptions. They monitor platform conditions, ensure clear door operations, and conduct safety checks to prevent accidents, injuries, or unauthorized access to subway tracks. Operators communicate emergency procedures, evacuate passengers during emergencies, and collaborate with transit authorities, emergency responders, or law enforcement agencies to ensure public safety and crisis management on metro trains.

Emergency Response and Protocol

Metro operators respond to emergencies, incidents, or technical failures affecting subway operations, promptly notifying transit control centers, and implementing emergency procedures to safeguard passengers and mitigate risks. They perform emergency braking maneuvers, coordinate evacuation procedures, and communicate critical information to passengers during emergency situations or service disruptions. Operators undergo emergency response training, first aid certification, and crisis management drills to enhance preparedness, response capabilities, and passenger safety in diverse subway operational environments.

Maintenance and Operational Checks

Conducting pre-operational checks, inspecting subway train systems, and reporting mechanical issues are essential responsibilities for metro operators to ensure train reliability, operational readiness, and compliance with safety standards. They perform routine inspections, check train brakes, doors, and control systems, and address minor mechanical issues to maintain optimal train performance and passenger comfort during subway operations. Operators collaborate with maintenance teams, engineers, or technicians to conduct scheduled maintenance tasks, troubleshoot technical problems, and ensure seamless metro service operations.

Customer Service and Communication

Providing courteous customer service, answering passenger inquiries, and addressing passenger concerns are integral aspects of metro operators' roles in enhancing commuter satisfaction and maintaining positive passenger experiences. Operators assist passengers with fare payment, route information, or transit directions, ensuring clear communication and efficient service delivery on metro trains. They foster a respectful environment, promote passenger etiquette, and facilitate orderly boarding and disembarkation processes to enhance passenger comfort, reduce congestion, and promote efficient subway travel experiences for commuters.

Operational Efficiency and Performance

Metro operators optimize train operations, adhere to transit schedules, and minimize service disruptions to achieve operational efficiency and maintain service reliability within metro rail networks. They monitor train performance metrics, track on-time performance, and implement strategies to improve train punctuality, reduce dwell times, and enhance overall transit system efficiency. Operators collaborate with transit management, dispatchers, or operational staff to address service delays, implement service adjustments, and optimize train scheduling to meet commuter demand and enhance metro service reliability.

Safety Regulations and Compliance

Adhering to safety regulations, operational protocols, and transit policies is essential for metro operators to ensure compliance with industry standards, promote safe subway operations, and protect passenger well-being during transit service delivery. Operators follow safety procedures, enforce passenger conduct rules, and monitor platform behavior to maintain orderliness, mitigate risks, and prevent safety incidents within metro stations and train environments. They participate in safety training programs, adhere to operational guidelines, and uphold transit regulations to uphold public trust and ensure regulatory compliance in subway operations.

Technology Integration and Innovation

Metro operators leverage technology advancements, train control systems, and communication tools to enhance operational efficiency, track train movements, and improve passenger information dissemination within metro rail networks. They utilize onboard computer systems, train management software, or real-time data analytics to monitor train operations, track service performance metrics, and optimize train routing for timely service delivery. Operators embrace digital innovations, implement passenger information displays, and integrate mobile apps to provide real-time updates, service alerts, and transit information to commuters, enhancing communication transparency and commuter satisfaction.

Career Development and Industry advancement

A career as a metro operator offers opportunities for career development, professional growth, and advancement within the transit industry. Operators may pursue advanced training in railway operations, transit management, or rail safety certifications to enhance job skills, expand career opportunities, and qualify for promotional roles within metro transit agencies or railway corporations. Professional development programs, leadership training initiatives, or specialized certifications enable operators to develop expertise, advance career goals, and contribute to operational excellence in subway transportation services.

Personal Perspectives

Personal narratives from metro operators provide firsthand insights about their experiences of serving as essential frontline workers in the urban transit industry. Operators share stories of navigating subway routes, interacting with diverse commuters, and contributing to seamless metro operations during peak travel periods or special events. They reflect on the satisfaction of ensuring public transportation access, promoting urban mobility, and delivering reliable metro services that support community connectivity and enhance the quality of life for city residents.

Chapter 19. Military Vehicle Drivers

Military vehicle drivers play a pivotal role in supporting military operations, ensuring logistical readiness, and enhancing operational capabilities within military transportation units. Through their dedication to mission readiness, adherence to operational standards, and commitment to service excellence, military drivers contribute to combat effectiveness, support national defense priorities, and uphold the mission success of military forces deployed worldwide.

Roles and Responsibilities
Military vehicle drivers play a crucial role in transporting personnel, equipment, and supplies within military operations, training exercises, or logistical missions. Their primary responsibilities include operating various military vehicles, adhering to tactical convoy procedures, and navigating diverse terrains or combat zones while ensuring mission readiness, operational security, and personnel safety. Military drivers support mission objectives, maintain vehicle readiness, and execute transport operations to facilitate military logistics, troop movements, or humanitarian aid missions in challenging and dynamic operational environments.

Vehicle Operation and Maintenance
Military drivers operate a wide range of specialized military vehicles, including trucks, armored personnel carriers, and tactical utility vehicles, equipped with advanced communications systems, defensive capabilities, and mission-specific equipment. They undergo specialized training in vehicle operation, tactical maneuvering, and defensive driving techniques to navigate rugged terrain, adverse weather conditions, or combat zones while ensuring vehicle performance, operational reliability, and mission

success. Drivers conduct pre-mission inspections, perform preventive maintenance checks, and address mechanical issues to sustain vehicle readiness and operational effectiveness during military deployments.

Convoy Operations and Tactical Movements

Conducting convoy operations, coordinating vehicle formations, and executing tactical movements are critical responsibilities for military drivers to support troop deployments, supply convoys, or logistical support missions. They follow convoy procedures, maintain operational security, and adhere to tactical protocols to mitigate risks, avoid ambushes, and ensure safe passage of personnel and equipment in hostile environments. Drivers communicate with convoy leaders, monitor radio communications, and implement defensive measures to protect convoy assets, maintain situational awareness, and respond to emergent threats or combat scenarios during military operations.

Combat and Emergency Response

Military drivers operate under combat conditions, execute emergency response protocols, and support battlefield logistics to sustain operational tempo and combat readiness for military units. They transport troops, evacuate casualties, or deliver critical supplies under fire, providing timely support to frontline units, medical personnel, or combat engineers during tactical engagements or humanitarian assistance missions. Drivers perform rapid response maneuvers, navigate hazardous conditions, and coordinate with combat units to facilitate troop movements, reinforce battlefield positions, and ensure mission success in dynamic operational environments.

Security and Force Protection

Ensuring vehicle security, enforcing operational security measures, and implementing force protection protocols are essential duties for military drivers to safeguard personnel, equipment, and mission-critical assets during military operations or security patrols. They conduct vehicle searches, inspect cargo, and enforce access control procedures to prevent unauthorized access, detect hostile threats, and maintain perimeter security in tactical environments. Drivers collaborate with security forces, monitor threat levels, and respond to security incidents to enhance force protection, mitigate risks, and uphold operational integrity in high-threat environments.

Logistical Support and Supply Chain Management

Providing logistical support, managing supply chains, and facilitating equipment transportation are integral roles for military drivers to sustain operational logistics, maintain mission readiness, and support sustained combat operations. They coordinate with logistics personnel, supply officers, or quartermaster units to transport ammunition, provisions, or specialized equipment to frontline units, forward operating bases, or logistical hubs. Drivers prioritize cargo handling, load securement, and inventory management to ensure timely delivery, operational continuity, and sustained combat support capabilities for military forces deployed in theater.

Communication and Mission Coordination

Maintaining communication, coordinating mission logistics, and facilitating information exchange are critical functions for military drivers to support command directives, tactical objectives, and operational planning during military deployments. They use radio communications, digital messaging systems, or satellite technologies to relay mission updates, report operational status, and coordinate convoy movements with command authorities or operational control centers. Drivers maintain situational awareness, adhere to mission orders, and adapt to changing operational requirements to achieve mission success, enhance operational effectiveness, and support joint military operations in complex operational environments.

Training and Skill Development

Military drivers undergo rigorous training programs, tactical proficiency exercises, and mission-specific training modules to enhance driving skills, tactical proficiency, and operational readiness for military vehicle operations. They participate in driver certification courses, combat training simulations, or live-fire exercises to refine vehicle handling techniques, improve tactical decision-making, and prepare for operational challenges encountered during military missions. Drivers engage in continuous skill development, receive feedback from training evaluations, and adapt to evolving mission requirements to maintain readiness and effectiveness as professional military drivers.

Career Advancement and Professional Growth

A career as a military vehicle driver offers opportunities for career advancement, specialized training, and professional development within military service branches or specialized units. Drivers may pursue advanced certifications in vehicle operation, logistics management, or specialized combat support roles to qualify for leadership positions, tactical command roles, or specialized technical assignments within military transportation units. Professional development programs, leadership courses, or advanced education opportunities enable drivers to expand skill sets, achieve career goals, and contribute to mission success in diverse military operational environments.

Personal Perspectives

Personal narratives from military drivers provide firsthand insights of their experiences of serving as essential personnel in military transportation units. Drivers share stories of navigating operational challenges, supporting combat missions, and contributing to military logistics operations in austere environments or during humanitarian missions. They reflect on the honor of serving their country, supporting fellow service members, and maintaining mission readiness to uphold national security, defend strategic interests, and achieve operational objectives in global military operations.

Chapter 20. Motorcycle Couriers

Motorcycle couriers play a pivotal role in urban logistics, providing fast and efficient delivery services, supporting business operations, and meeting customer demands for timely transportation solutions. Through their commitment to delivery excellence, adherence to safety standards, and adoption of technology-driven solutions, motorcycle couriers enhance service reliability, promote environmental sustainability, and contribute to the dynamic evolution of urban delivery networks in response to changing consumer preferences and market demands.

Roles and Responsibilities
Motorcycle couriers, also known as bike messengers or delivery riders, specialize in transporting documents, parcels, or goods quickly and efficiently across urban areas using motorcycles or scooters. Their primary responsibilities include navigating city streets, adhering to delivery schedules, and ensuring the timely and secure delivery of items to designated recipients. Motorcycle couriers play a critical role in providing expedited delivery services, supporting logistics operations, and meeting customer demands for swift transportation solutions in densely populated urban environments.

Navigating Urban Environments
Motorcycle couriers navigate through congested city streets, alleys, or pedestrian zones to deliver documents, packages, or food orders to residential or business addresses. They utilize knowledge of local routes, traffic patterns, and shortcuts to optimize delivery routes, minimize travel time, and maintain efficient delivery operations. Couriers prioritize safe riding practices, observe traffic regulations, and maneuver through urban

traffic to ensure timely and reliable delivery of goods while promoting road safety and minimizing delivery delays.

Parcel Handling and Delivery

Handling parcels, packages, or sensitive documents securely is essential for motorcycle couriers to protect items from damage, loss, or theft during transit. They use secure storage compartments, protective packaging, or delivery bags to safeguard items, prevent moisture or weather damage, and ensure the integrity of delivered goods. Couriers verify recipient information, obtain delivery confirmations, and maintain accurate records to track parcel movements, manage delivery schedules, and provide proof of delivery to customers or dispatchers.

Customer Service and Communication

Providing exceptional customer service, responding to delivery inquiries, and addressing customer concerns are integral aspects of motorcycle couriers' roles in enhancing customer satisfaction and maintaining positive client relationships. Couriers communicate delivery statuses, update customers on delivery progress, and accommodate special delivery requests to meet customer preferences or delivery instructions. They promote courteous interaction, resolve delivery issues promptly, and uphold service standards to enhance customer loyalty and support business growth in the competitive delivery service industry.

Delivery Efficiency and Time Management

Efficient delivery performance and effective time management are critical for motorcycle couriers to meet delivery deadlines, optimize delivery routes, and fulfill customer expectations for fast and reliable delivery services. They prioritize delivery schedules, coordinate multiple deliveries, and use mobile apps or GPS navigation tools to plan efficient routes, track delivery progress, and ensure on-time delivery of parcels or documents. Couriers adapt to changing traffic conditions, weather challenges, or logistical constraints to maintain delivery efficiency and enhance service reliability for customers.

Safety and Risk Management
Maintaining safety awareness, adhering to motorcycle safety protocols, and mitigating delivery risks are paramount for motorcycle couriers to prevent accidents, ensure personal safety, and protect delivered goods during transit. They wear protective gear, helmets, or reflective clothing, conduct pre-ride safety inspections, and practice defensive riding techniques to navigate urban traffic, avoid collisions, and minimize injury risks while delivering items. Couriers assess delivery environments, anticipate potential hazards, and respond to emergency situations to promote rider safety and ensure incident-free delivery operations.

Environmental Impact and Sustainability
Motorcycle couriers support environmental sustainability initiatives, promote eco-friendly delivery practices, and reduce carbon emissions associated with urban transportation. They use fuel-efficient motorcycles, electric scooters, or alternative energy vehicles to minimize environmental footprint, conserve natural resources, and contribute to sustainable logistics solutions within urban delivery networks. Couriers advocate for green delivery initiatives, adopt recyclable packaging materials, and implement waste reduction strategies to support environmental stewardship and promote sustainable business practices in the delivery service industry.

Technology Integration and Digital Solutions
Integrating technology solutions, leveraging mobile apps, and utilizing digital platforms enhance operational efficiency, streamline delivery processes, and improve communication for motorcycle couriers. They use smartphone apps for route navigation, real-time delivery tracking, and customer communication to optimize delivery operations, provide instant updates on delivery statuses,

and enhance transparency in delivery services. Couriers embrace digital innovations, utilize electronic payment systems, and leverage data analytics to enhance service capabilities, improve delivery performance, and meet evolving customer demands in the digital age.

Career Development and Professional Growth

A career as a motorcycle courier offers opportunities for professional development, skill enhancement, and career advancement within the delivery service industry. Couriers may pursue training in safe riding practices, customer service excellence, or logistical management to expand job skills, qualify for specialized delivery roles, or advance to supervisory positions within delivery companies or courier services. Professional development programs, leadership training initiatives, or continuing education opportunities enable couriers to enhance career prospects, achieve career goals, and contribute to service excellence in urban delivery operations.

Personal Perspectives

Personal narratives from motorcycle couriers provide firsthand insights about their experiences of serving as essential delivery personnel in urban environments. Couriers share stories of navigating through city traffic, delivering urgent packages, and overcoming logistical challenges to meet customer expectations and deadlines. They reflect on the satisfaction of providing reliable delivery services, building customer trust, and contributing to efficient logistics operations that support urban mobility, business productivity, and community connectivity through expedited delivery solutions.

Chapter 21. Paratransit Drivers

Paratransit drivers play a vital role in providing accessible transportation, enhancing mobility options, and supporting community inclusion for individuals with disabilities. Through their dedication to passenger assistance, adherence to safety standards, and commitment to service excellence, paratransit drivers contribute to equitable access, promote inclusive transportation services, and empower individuals with disabilities to navigate daily life with dignity, independence, and confidence.

Roles and Responsibilities

Paratransit drivers provide transportation services for individuals with disabilities or special needs, ensuring safe and reliable travel to medical appointments, work, school, and other essential destinations. They assist passengers with boarding and disembarking vehicles, secure mobility aids such as wheelchairs or walkers, and ensure passenger comfort and safety throughout the journey. Paratransit drivers play a critical role in enhancing accessibility, independence, and mobility options for individuals with diverse mobility challenges within their communities.

Passenger Assistance and Support

Paratransit drivers offer personalized assistance, sensitivity, and support to passengers with disabilities or mobility limitations, ensuring respectful and dignified transportation experiences. They communicate effectively with passengers, address specific needs or preferences, and provide physical assistance, if required, to facilitate safe vehicle entry and exit. Drivers maintain rapport, engage with passengers in conversation, and promote a supportive environment to enhance passenger confidence, comfort, and the overall travel experience.

Vehicle Accessibility and Safety

Ensuring vehicle accessibility and maintaining safety standards are paramount for paratransit drivers to accommodate passengers with disabilities or medical conditions effectively. They operate accessible vehicles equipped with wheelchair lifts, ramps, securement systems, and accessibility features to facilitate seamless boarding, secure mobility devices, and ensure passenger safety during transit. Drivers conduct pre-trip vehicle inspections, verify equipment functionality, and adhere to safety protocols to prevent accidents, minimize risks, and promote safe travel conditions for passengers with diverse mobility needs.

Route Navigation and Efficiency

Navigating diverse routes, adhering to service schedules, and optimizing travel routes are essential responsibilities for paratransit drivers to ensure on-time arrival, efficient service delivery, and reliable transportation for passengers with disabilities. They utilize GPS navigation systems, route planning tools, and local knowledge to navigate traffic patterns, avoid congestion, and select accessible routes that accommodate passenger destinations, preferences, or medical appointments. Drivers prioritize punctuality, adhere to transit schedules, and adjust travel routes to accommodate passenger requests or unexpected travel disruptions effectively.

Regulatory Compliance and Passenger Rights

Adhering to regulatory requirements, transit policies, and passenger rights is fundamental for paratransit drivers to ensure compliance with accessibility laws, protect passenger rights, and uphold service quality standards. They undergo training on disability awareness, ADA regulations, and passenger assistance techniques to promote inclusive transportation practices, accommodate diverse passenger needs, and safeguard passenger rights during transit. Drivers advocate for passenger rights, provide information on accessible transportation options, and facilitate accessible service delivery to promote equitable access and support for individuals with disabilities within transportation networks.

Customer Service Excellence

Delivering exceptional customer service, addressing passenger inquiries, and resolving service issues are integral aspects of paratransit drivers' roles in enhancing passenger satisfaction and fostering positive travel experiences. They maintain a professional demeanor, respond to passenger feedback, and handle service inquiries or complaints with empathy, patience, and proactive resolution to ensure customer satisfaction. Drivers promote courteous interaction, uphold service standards, and strive to exceed passenger expectations by providing reliable, respectful, and accommodating transportation services for individuals with disabilities.

Emergency Response and Crisis Management

Paratransit drivers respond to emergencies, medical incidents, or unforeseen events affecting passenger safety or service operations, demonstrating readiness to implement emergency procedures, notify emergency services, and provide immediate assistance to passengers in distress. They undergo emergency response training, first aid certification, and crisis management drills to enhance preparedness, address medical emergencies, and ensure passenger well-being during transit. Drivers collaborate with emergency responders, transit authorities, or medical personnel to coordinate emergency interventions, support passenger evacuation, and mitigate risks in critical situations affecting paratransit services.

Technology Integration and Service Innovation

Integrating technology solutions, leveraging mobile applications, and utilizing digital platforms enhance operational efficiency, optimize service delivery, and improve communication for paratransit drivers. They use mobile apps for trip scheduling, real-time vehicle tracking, and passenger communication to streamline service operations, provide trip updates, and enhance service reliability. Drivers embrace digital innovations, adopt accessible technology solutions, and leverage data analytics to improve service accessibility, accommodate passenger preferences, and promote inclusive transportation options for individuals with disabilities.

Career Development and Professional Growth

A career as a paratransit driver offers opportunities for career advancement, specialized training, and professional development within the transportation service sector. Drivers may pursue certifications in passenger safety, ADA compliance, or specialized vehicle operation to expand job skills, qualify for leadership roles, or advance to supervisory positions within paratransit service providers or transit agencies. Professional development programs, ongoing training initiatives, or continuing education opportunities enable drivers to enhance service capabilities, achieve career goals, and contribute to inclusive transportation solutions that support mobility and accessibility for individuals with disabilities.

Personal Perspectives

Paratransit drivers share stories of assisting passengers, overcoming transportation barriers, and promoting independent mobility for individuals with disabilities within their communities.

They reflect on the fulfillment of supporting passenger independence, delivering compassionate care, and making a meaningful difference in the lives of individuals who rely on paratransit services for essential travel needs.

Chapter 22. Police Car Drivers

Police car drivers play a critical role in law enforcement efforts to ensure public safety, enforce laws, and protect community well-being through proactive patrols, emergency response readiness, and community engagement strategies. Through their dedication to service excellence, adherence to professional standards, and commitment to public safety, police car drivers uphold the responsibilities of safeguarding communities, promoting justice, and maintaining public trust in law enforcement agencies that serve and protect diverse communities nationwide.

Roles and Responsibilities
Police car drivers, often known as patrol officers, are responsible for maintaining public safety, enforcing laws, and responding to emergencies within their jurisdictions. They operate police vehicles with precision and urgency, conduct patrols to deter crime, and respond swiftly to incidents such as accidents, disturbances, or criminal activities. Police car drivers play a crucial role in law enforcement efforts to protect communities, ensure traffic safety, and uphold public order through proactive patrols, emergency response readiness, and effective communication with dispatchers and fellow officers.

Vehicle Operation and Tactical Driving
Police car drivers undergo specialized training in vehicle operation, tactical driving techniques, and emergency vehicle handling to navigate urban streets, highways, or challenging terrains safely and effectively. They use advanced driving skills, including pursuit driving, defensive maneuvers, and evasive techniques, to pursue suspects, respond to emergencies, or provide support to fellow officers during high-risk situations. Drivers prioritize safety, adhere

to traffic laws, and maintain control of police vehicles while ensuring rapid response capabilities and operational readiness to support law enforcement operations.

Law Enforcement Support and Incident Response

Supporting law enforcement operations, responding to emergencies, and providing backup to officers are primary duties for police car drivers to maintain public safety, enforce laws, and protect community members. They respond to calls for service, conduct proactive patrols, and intervene in criminal activities, traffic violations, or public disturbances to maintain order, resolve incidents, and ensure compliance with legal statutes. Drivers collaborate with law enforcement agencies, communicate effectively with dispatchers, and coordinate responses to emergency situations to safeguard lives, property, and public welfare.

Emergency Response Protocols

Police car drivers implement emergency response protocols, prioritize urgent calls, and navigate traffic or hazardous conditions to reach incident scenes promptly. They use sirens, lights, and communication systems to signal emergency response, clear traffic lanes, and expedite travel while ensuring the safety of pedestrians, motorists, and fellow officers. Drivers assess situations, deploy resources, and coordinate with emergency services to manage crises, stabilize incident scenes, and provide immediate assistance to victims, witnesses, or vulnerable individuals requiring law enforcement intervention.

Community Engagement and Public Relations

Engaging with the community, fostering positive relationships, and promoting public trust are integral aspects of police car drivers' roles in enhancing community policing efforts and building rapport with residents. They participate in community outreach programs, public safety initiatives, or neighborhood watch activities to educate residents, address public concerns, and promote crime prevention strategies. Drivers engage in respectful interactions, demonstrate empathy, and uphold ethical standards to enhance transparency, foster community cooperation, and strengthen partnerships that support collaborative crime prevention and public safety initiatives.

Evidence Handling and Crime Scene Management

Managing evidence, securing crime scenes, and preserving forensic integrity are critical responsibilities for police car drivers to support criminal investigations, gather evidence, and uphold legal procedures. They document incident details, collect physical evidence, and maintain a chain of custody to support investigative processes, criminal prosecutions, or judicial proceedings. Drivers adhere to evidence handling protocols, coordinate with forensic specialists, and collaborate with detectives to ensure thorough documentation, accurate reporting, and lawful procedures in managing crime scenes and supporting investigative efforts.

Crisis Intervention and Conflict Resolution

Police car drivers engage in crisis intervention, de-escalation techniques, and conflict resolution strategies to defuse tense situations, manage interpersonal conflicts, and promote peaceful resolutions during law enforcement interactions. They assess behavioral cues, communicate effectively with individuals in distress, and use verbal persuasion to mitigate risks, prevent escalation, and resolve disputes peacefully. Drivers exercise discretion, apply crisis intervention tactics, and uphold professional conduct to maintain public safety, protect individual rights, and foster positive outcomes in challenging law enforcement encounters.

Training and Skill Development

Continual training, skill enhancement, and professional development are essential for police car drivers to maintain proficiency in law enforcement practices, tactical operations, and emergency response readiness. They participate in ongoing training programs, tactical simulations, or scenario-based exercises to refine driving skills, enhance decision-making abilities, and adapt to evolving law enforcement challenges. Drivers pursue specialized certifications, attend leadership courses, or acquire advanced training in specialized units to qualify for specialized assignments, career advancement opportunities, or leadership roles within law enforcement agencies.

Safety and Officer Wellness

Prioritizing officer safety, maintaining physical wellness, and promoting mental resilience are priorities for police car drivers to sustain operational readiness, manage occupational stressors, and ensure long-term career effectiveness. They practice physical fitness routines, engage in wellness programs, and access mental health resources to support overall well-being, mitigate job-related stress, and enhance personal resilience in demanding law enforcement environments. Drivers advocate for peer support, cultivate teamwork, and prioritize safety protocols to safeguard officer health, enhance job satisfaction, and promote sustainable career longevity in the law enforcement profession.

Community Safety and Public Trust

Police car drivers uphold principles of integrity, accountability, and ethical conduct to build public trust, promote community safety, and uphold law enforcement standards that prioritize service, protection, and justice for all community members. They demonstrate commitment to ethical policing, uphold constitutional rights, and enforce laws impartially to maintain public confidence in law enforcement institutions. Drivers engage in community dialogues, address citizen concerns, and collaborate with stakeholders to enhance transparency, accountability, and public trust in law enforcement practices that promote community safety and uphold societal values.

Chapter 23. Private Hire Drivers

Private hire drivers play a pivotal role in providing safe, reliable, and convenient transportation services for passengers through private hire companies or ride-hailing platforms. Through their commitment to passenger safety, service excellence, and operational efficiency, private hire drivers enhance mobility options, support urban transportation needs, and contribute to customer satisfaction in the evolving landscape of private hire transportation services.

Roles and Responsibilities
Private-hire drivers provide transportation services for passengers by pre-booking through private-hire companies or ride-hailing platforms. They operate vehicles such as cars or minivans, pick up passengers from specified locations, and transport them to their destinations in a safe and timely manner. Private-hire drivers prioritize passenger comfort, adhere to traffic regulations, and ensure reliable transportation services while maintaining professionalism and customer service excellence.

Passenger Service and Safety
Private-hire drivers prioritize passenger safety, provide courteous service, and ensure a comfortable travel experience for passengers. They assist passengers with luggage, offer door-to-door service, and maintain cleanliness and hygiene in their vehicles. Drivers adhere to safety protocols, secure seat belts, and implement necessary safety measures to protect passenger health and well-being during travel. Private-hire drivers communicate effectively with passengers, respond to inquiries, and accommodate special requests to enhance customer satisfaction and promote positive passenger experiences.

Navigating Routes and Traffic Conditions
Navigating diverse routes, avoiding traffic congestion, and selecting optimal travel routes are essential responsibilities for private hire drivers to ensure efficient transportation services and on-time arrivals for passengers. They use GPS navigation systems, map apps, or local knowledge to plan routes, monitor traffic conditions, and adapt travel routes to minimize travel time and optimize passenger convenience. Drivers maintain situational awareness, anticipate traffic challenges, and utilize alternative routes to avoid delays and ensure punctual transportation services for passengers.

Vehicle Maintenance and Care
Maintaining vehicle cleanliness, conducting regular inspections, and ensuring vehicle maintenance are crucial for private hire drivers to uphold vehicle safety, reliability, and operational efficiency. They perform pre-trip vehicle checks, monitor fluid levels, and inspect vehicle tires, brakes, and lighting systems to ensure safe vehicle operation. Drivers adhere to maintenance schedules, address mechanical issues promptly, and collaborate with vehicle service providers to maintain optimal vehicle performance and ensure passenger safety throughout their journeys.

Customer Relations and Service Excellence
Providing superior customer service, addressing passenger needs, and fostering positive relationships are fundamental aspects of private-hire drivers' roles in promoting customer satisfaction and loyalty. They greet passengers courteously, engage in friendly conversation, and create a welcoming atmosphere to enhance passenger comfort and confidence during travel. Drivers accommodate passenger preferences, offer personalized service, and resolve service inquiries or concerns promptly to maintain high service standards and uphold the reputation of private hire companies or ride-hailing platforms.

Payment Processing and Financial Transactions

Facilitating payment transactions, processing fares, and handling financial transactions are critical responsibilities for private hire drivers to ensure accurate billing, secure transactions, and efficient payment processing for passengers. They utilize mobile payment apps, electronic payment systems, or cash handling procedures to collect fares, issue receipts, and provide payment options that accommodate passenger preferences or payment methods. Drivers maintain financial records, reconcile daily transactions, and comply with company policies or regulatory requirements governing fare collection and financial accountability in private-hire transportation services.

Regulatory Compliance and Licensing

Adhering to regulatory requirements, obtaining necessary licenses, and complying with transportation laws are essential for private-hire drivers to operate legally and maintain regulatory compliance in the transportation industry. They acquire commercial driver's licenses, undergo background checks, and obtain permits or endorsements required by local authorities or transportation agencies to operate as private hire drivers. Drivers stay informed about regulatory updates, adhere to transportation regulations, and uphold industry standards to ensure lawful operation, protect passenger rights, and promote public safety in private-hire transportation services.

Emergency Response and Crisis Management

Private hire drivers respond to emergencies, assist passengers in distress, and manage crisis situations to ensure passenger safety and well-being during travel. They undergo training in emergency response protocols, first aid procedures, or crisis management techniques to handle medical emergencies, traffic incidents, or unexpected situations affecting passenger safety. Drivers communicate with emergency services, provide assistance to injured passengers, and coordinate responses with law enforcement or medical personnel to facilitate timely interventions and mitigate risks in emergency situations encountered during private hire services.

Technology Integration and Digital Solutions

Integrating technology solutions, leveraging mobile apps, and utilizing digital platforms enhance operational efficiency, streamline service delivery, and improve communication for private hire drivers. They use ride-hailing apps for trip scheduling, real-time navigation, and passenger communication to optimize service operations, provide updates on trip statuses, and enhance passenger connectivity during travel. Drivers embrace digital innovations, adopt GPS tracking systems, and leverage data analytics to improve service reliability, accommodate passenger preferences, and enhance overall travel experiences in the private hire transportation sector.

Career Development and Professional Growth

A career as a private hire driver offers opportunities for career advancement, skill development, and professional growth within the transportation service industry. Drivers may pursue training in customer service excellence, defensive driving techniques, or vehicle operation to enhance job skills, qualify for specialized roles, or advance to supervisory positions within private hire companies or ride-hailing platforms. Professional development programs, leadership training initiatives, or continuing education opportunities enable drivers to expand career prospects, achieve career goals, and contribute to service excellence in private-hire transportation services.

Personal Perspectives

Private hire drivers share stories of navigating city traffic, interacting with passengers, and overcoming logistical challenges to deliver reliable transportation services. They reflect on the satisfaction of meeting passenger needs, building customer trust, and contributing to efficient mobility solutions that support urban transportation networks and meet diverse passenger travel demands in the private hire transportation industry.

Chapter 24. Public Transportation Drivers

Public transportation drivers play a vital role in urban mobility, community connectivity, and sustainable transportation solutions through their dedication to passenger safety, service excellence, and operational efficiency in public transit operations. Through their commitment to professionalism, adherence to regulatory standards, and advocacy for inclusive transportation practices, public transportation drivers contribute to enhancing public transit services, promoting community well-being, and supporting equitable access to transportation resources for passengers in diverse urban environments.

Roles and Responsibilities
Public transportation drivers provide essential transportation services to passengers using buses, trains, trams, or other public transit vehicles. They ensure safe boarding and disembarking of passengers, operate vehicles along designated routes, and adhere to scheduled timetables to facilitate reliable transportation services. Public transportation drivers prioritize passenger safety, maintain professional conduct, and uphold service standards while promoting efficient urban mobility and supporting public transportation infrastructure.

Passenger Safety and Assistance
Public transportation drivers prioritize passenger safety by enforcing safety protocols, securing vehicle doors, and assisting passengers with disabilities or mobility limitations during boarding and disembarking. They communicate safety instructions, ensure compliance with transit regulations, and monitor passenger behavior to maintain a secure environment onboard public transit vehicles. Drivers provide courteous assistance, address

passenger inquiries, and intervene in emergencies to ensure passenger well-being and uphold safety standards throughout travel.

Route Navigation and Transit Operations

Navigating established routes, adhering to traffic regulations, and optimizing travel schedules are essential responsibilities for public transportation drivers to ensure efficient transit operations and on-time service delivery. They use route maps, GPS navigation systems, or transit control centers to navigate traffic conditions, minimize delays, and maintain adherence to scheduled timetables while accommodating passenger travel needs. Drivers communicate with dispatchers, coordinate service adjustments, and respond to service disruptions to enhance operational efficiency and support seamless public transportation services for passengers.

Customer Service Excellence

Delivering exceptional customer service, fostering positive passenger experiences, and promoting public transit ridership are fundamental aspects of public transportation drivers' roles in enhancing passenger satisfaction and loyalty. They greet passengers courteously, provide route information, and assist with fare collection or ticket validation to facilitate smooth travel experiences. Drivers engage in professional interactions, address passenger concerns, and resolve service issues promptly to promote positive perceptions of public transportation services and encourage repeat ridership among passengers.

Vehicle Maintenance and Safety checks

Maintaining vehicle cleanliness, conducting pre-trip inspections, and ensuring mechanical readiness are critical for public transportation drivers to uphold vehicle safety, reliability, and operational efficiency. They perform daily vehicle checks, monitor fluid levels, and inspect vehicle components such as brakes, tires, and lighting systems to ensure safe vehicle operation. Drivers report maintenance issues, collaborate with maintenance staff, and adhere to preventive maintenance schedules to prevent mechanical failures, enhance passenger safety, and maintain service reliability in public transportation operations.

Accessibility and Inclusivity

Promoting accessibility, accommodating diverse passenger needs, and supporting inclusive transportation services are priorities for public transportation drivers to ensure equitable access and support mobility for passengers with disabilities or special needs. They operate accessible vehicles, deploy wheelchair ramps or lifts, and provide assistance to passengers with mobility aids or visual impairments to facilitate barrier-free travel experiences. Drivers undergo disability awareness training, adhere to accessibility laws, and advocate for passenger rights to promote inclusive transportation solutions that enhance community mobility and support universal access for all passengers.

Emergency Response and Crisis Management

Public transportation drivers respond to emergencies, implement crisis management protocols, and ensure passenger safety during unforeseen incidents or service disruptions. They undergo emergency response training, first aid certification, or crisis intervention techniques to handle medical emergencies, accidents, or security incidents affecting passenger safety. Drivers communicate with emergency services, coordinate passenger evacuation procedures, and facilitate timely interventions to mitigate risks, restore service operations, and support passenger well-being during emergency situations encountered in public transportation services.

Environmental Sustainability and Green Initiatives

Supporting environmental sustainability, promoting eco-friendly transportation practices, and reducing carbon footprints are priorities for public transportation drivers to contribute to environmental stewardship and sustainable urban mobility solutions. They adhere to eco-driving principles, optimize fuel efficiency, and minimize vehicle emissions during transit operations to conserve natural resources and mitigate environmental impacts. Drivers participate in eco-friendly initiatives, support public transit policies, and advocate for green transportation practices that promote energy conservation, air quality improvement, and environmental sustainability in public transportation networks.

Regulatory Compliance and Transit Policies

Adhering to regulatory requirements, complying with transit policies, and upholding passenger rights are essential for public transportation drivers to operate lawfully, maintain service integrity, and ensure quality service delivery. They acquire commercial driver's licenses, undergo background checks, and obtain certifications or endorsements required by transit authorities or regulatory agencies to perform public transportation duties. Drivers stay informed about transit regulations, enforce fare policies, and uphold ethical standards to protect passenger rights, maintain public trust, and promote responsible transit operations in urban transportation networks.

Career Development and Professional Growth

A career as a public transportation driver offers opportunities for career advancement, skill development, and professional growth within the transportation service sector. Drivers may pursue training in customer service excellence, defensive driving techniques, or transit management to enhance job skills, qualify for leadership roles, or advance to supervisory positions within transit agencies or public transportation providers. Professional development programs, ongoing training initiatives, or continuing education opportunities enable drivers to expand career prospects, achieve career goals, and contribute to service excellence in public transportation services.

Personal Perspectives
Public transportation drivers share stories of navigating city routes, interacting with diverse passengers, and overcoming operational challenges to deliver reliable transportation services. They reflect on the importance of promoting public trust, supporting community mobility, and contributing to urban transit networks that provide accessible, safe, and efficient transportation solutions for passengers in cities and metropolitan areas.

Chapter 25. Racing Drivers

Racing drivers exemplify dedication, skill, and resilience in competitive motorsport disciplines through their pursuit of race victories, championship titles, and contributions to global racing legacies. Through their commitment to racing excellence, technical proficiency, and strategic race craft, racing drivers inspire motorsport enthusiasts, promote sporting achievements, and elevate the excitement of motorsport competitions worldwide.

Roles and Responsibilities

Racing drivers are skilled professionals who compete in various motorsport disciplines, including Formula 1, NASCAR, rally racing, and endurance events. They showcase exceptional driving abilities, tactical race strategies, and physical endurance to excel in competitive racing environments. Racing drivers participate in qualifying sessions, adhere to race regulations, and demonstrate precision, agility, and focus during high-speed competitions to achieve podium finishes and championship titles.

Vehicle Dynamics and Racing Techniques

Mastering vehicle dynamics, employing racing techniques, and optimizing performance are essential for racing drivers to navigate race tracks, corners, and straights effectively. They utilize advanced driving skills, including braking techniques, cornering speeds, and throttle control, to maintain optimal vehicle traction, maximize acceleration, and minimize lap times during racing competitions. Drivers adapt racing strategies, assess track conditions, and implement tire management strategies to optimize vehicle handling and achieve competitive advantages in challenging racing environments.

Team Collaboration and Pit Stop Coordination

Collaborating with race teams, communicating with engineers, and coordinating pit stops are crucial for racing drivers to maximize race performance, vehicle setup, and strategic race planning. They provide feedback on vehicle handling, discuss race strategies with engineers, and make real-time adjustments to vehicle settings during pit stops to optimize race performance and maintain competitive positions. Drivers rely on teamwork, pit crew support, and effective communication to execute seamless pit stop operations and ensure race strategy alignment for successful race outcomes.

Physical Fitness and Mental Preparedness
Maintaining peak physical fitness, mental acuity, and resilience are priorities for racing drivers to endure rigorous race conditions, sustain focus, and perform consistently throughout racing seasons. They engage in physical conditioning routines, cardio exercises, and strength training programs to enhance endurance, muscle stamina, and the reaction times required for high-speed racing maneuvers. Drivers practice mental preparation techniques, manage race-day pressures, and maintain concentration to stay alert, make split-second decisions, and respond swiftly to dynamic race situations during competitive racing events.

Risk Management and Safety Protocols
Prioritizing risk management, adhering to safety protocols, and promoting driver safety are fundamental for racing drivers to mitigate risks, prevent accidents, and ensure personal well-being during racing competitions. They undergo safety briefings, adhere to track regulations, and utilize safety equipment such as helmets, fire-resistant suits, and HANS devices to protect against injuries and enhance driver protection in high-speed racing environments. Drivers must maintain situational awareness, respect track limits, and exercise caution to uphold safety standards and promote responsible racing behaviors on race tracks.

Technological Advancements and Data Analysis
Leveraging technological advancements, analyzing race data, and using telemetry systems enhance racing drivers' ability to monitor vehicle performance, optimize race strategies, and improve lap times during competitive racing events. They utilize onboard telemetry systems, data loggers, and real-time analytics to assess vehicle dynamics, monitor engine performance, and analyze driver inputs to refine racing techniques and enhance race competitiveness. Drivers collaborate with engineers, interpret data insights, and implement performance enhancements to maximize race performance and achieve competitive advantages in motorsport disciplines.

Career Development and Professional Racing
Career development, pursuing racing championships, and advancing in professional racing careers are aspirations for racing drivers to achieve success, recognition, and championship titles in motorsport disciplines worldwide. They compete in racing series, progress through developmental leagues, and secure sponsorship opportunities to fund race programs, participate in prestigious events, and gain exposure on global racing circuits. Drivers cultivate racing skills, establish professional reputations, and pursue career milestones to elevate their profiles, attract team offers, and advance to elite racing categories or achieve championship victories in competitive motorsport competitions.

Fan Engagement and Media Relations
Engaging with fans, participating in media interactions, and promoting motorsport are integral aspects of racing drivers' roles in enhancing fan loyalty, expanding fan bases, and supporting motorsport growth. They interact with spectators, sign autographs, and participate in fan events to connect with supporters, cultivate fan loyalty, and promote motorsport enthusiasm worldwide. Drivers engage with media outlets, conduct interviews, and share race experiences to generate media coverage, increase visibility, and

enhance public awareness of motorsport achievements and contributions to the racing community.

Environmental Sustainability and Motorsport Innovation

Supporting environmental sustainability, advocating for eco-friendly initiatives, and promoting motorsport innovation are priorities for racing drivers to contribute to sustainability efforts and reduce carbon footprints in motorsport activities. They endorse eco-driving practices, support green technologies, and participate in sustainable racing initiatives to minimize environmental impacts, conserve natural resources, and promote eco-friendly practices in motorsport disciplines. Drivers collaborate with motorsport organizations, embrace innovation, and advocate for sustainable racing solutions that align with environmental stewardship principles and promote long-term sustainability in global motorsport industries.

Challenges and Rewards of Racing

Navigating challenges, embracing competition, and experiencing rewards are intrinsic to racing drivers' journeys in pursuing motorsport careers, achieving race successes, and overcoming adversities in competitive racing environments. They confront race challenges, manage performance pressures, and celebrate achievements, podium finishes, or championship victories as milestones in their racing careers. Drivers persevere through setbacks, embrace opportunities for growth, and cherish the exhilaration of racing experiences that define their passion, commitment, and dedication to motorsport excellence on and off the race track.

Chapter 26. Ride-Hailing Drivers

Ride-hailing drivers play a pivotal role in urban mobility, providing convenient, accessible, and reliable transportation services through ride-hailing platforms. Through their dedication to passenger safety, service excellence, and operational efficiency, ride-hailing drivers enhance transportation options, support urban mobility needs, and contribute to customer satisfaction in the evolving landscape of ride-hailing transportation services.

Roles and Responsibilities

Ride-hailing drivers provide on-demand transportation services through mobile apps for passengers seeking convenient and reliable travel options. They operate personal vehicles, pick up passengers from specified locations, and transport them to destinations while ensuring safety, comfort, and adherence to ride-hailing company policies. Ride-hailing drivers prioritize passenger satisfaction, navigate city streets, and maintain professionalism to deliver exceptional service experiences and foster positive customer relationships in the ride-hailing industry.

Passenger Service and Safety

Ensuring passenger safety, offering courteous service, and providing comfortable travel experiences are primary responsibilities for ride-hailing drivers. They greet passengers warmly, assist with luggage, and maintain clean and well-maintained vehicles to enhance passenger comfort and satisfaction. Drivers adhere to safety protocols, secure seat belts, and implement necessary safety measures to protect passenger health during travel. Ride-hailing drivers communicate effectively with passengers, address inquiries, and accommodate special requests to promote a positive and enjoyable ride-hailing experience for passengers.

Navigating Routes and Traffic Conditions
Navigating city routes, optimizing travel routes, and avoiding traffic congestion are essential for ride-hailing drivers to provide efficient transportation services and ensure on-time arrivals for passengers. They utilize GPS navigation systems, map apps, or local knowledge to plan travel routes, monitor traffic updates, and select alternative routes when necessary to minimize travel time and enhance passenger convenience. Drivers maintain awareness of traffic laws, adhere to road regulations, and adjust travel plans to accommodate passenger destinations and route preferences during ride-hailing services.

Vehicle Maintenance and Care
Maintaining vehicle cleanliness, conducting routine inspections, and ensuring vehicle readiness are critical for ride-hailing drivers to uphold vehicle safety, reliability, and operational efficiency. They perform pre-trip vehicle checks, monitor fluid levels, and inspect vehicle components such as brakes, tires, and lighting systems to ensure safe vehicle operation. Drivers adhere to maintenance schedules, address mechanical issues promptly, and collaborate with auto service providers to maintain optimal vehicle performance and safety standards in ride-hailing transportation services.

Customer Relations and Service Excellence
Delivering excellent customer service, fostering positive interactions, and building rapport with passengers are key aspects of ride-hailing drivers' roles in promoting customer satisfaction and loyalty. They engage passengers respectfully, communicate professionally, and provide information on ride details or travel updates to enhance passenger experience and satisfaction. Drivers address passenger concerns promptly, resolve service

issues efficiently, and ensure transparent communication to maintain trust and reliability in ride-hailing service delivery and support long-term customer relationships.

Payment Processing and Financial Transactions

Facilitating payment transactions, processing fares, and handling financial transactions accurately are essential responsibilities for ride-hailing drivers to ensure seamless payment experiences and financial accountability. They utilize mobile payment apps, electronic payment systems, or cash handling procedures to collect fares, issue receipts, and provide payment options that accommodate passenger preferences or payment methods. Drivers maintain financial records, reconcile transactions, and comply with ride-hailing company policies or regulatory requirements governing fare collection and financial management in ride-hailing transportation services.

Regulatory Compliance and Licensing

Adhering to regulatory requirements, obtaining necessary licenses, and complying with transportation laws are critical for ride-hailing drivers to operate legally and maintain regulatory compliance in the ride-hailing industry. They acquire commercial driver's licenses, undergo background checks, and obtain permits or endorsements required by local authorities or transportation agencies to provide ride-hailing services. Drivers stay informed about regulatory updates, adhere to transportation regulations, and uphold industry standards to ensure lawful operation, protect passenger rights, and promote public safety in ride-hailing transportation networks.

Emergency Response and Crisis Management

Responding to emergencies, managing crisis situations, and ensuring passenger safety during unforeseen incidents are priorities for ride-hailing drivers to uphold safety standards and mitigate risks in ride-hailing services. They undergo training in emergency response protocols, first aid procedures, or crisis management techniques to handle medical emergencies, accidents, or security incidents affecting passenger safety. Drivers communicate with emergency services, provide assistance to passengers in distress, and coordinate responses with law enforcement or medical personnel to facilitate timely interventions and support passenger well-being during emergency situations encountered in ride-hailing operations.

Technological Integration and Digital Solutions

Leveraging technology solutions, integrating mobile apps, and utilizing digital platforms enhance operational efficiency, streamline service delivery, and improve communication for ride-hailing drivers. They use ride-hailing apps for trip scheduling, real-time navigation, and passenger communication to optimize service operations, provide updates on trip statuses, and enhance passenger connectivity during travel. Drivers embrace digital innovations, adopt GPS tracking systems, and utilize data analytics to improve service reliability, accommodate passenger preferences, and enhance overall travel experiences in the ride-hailing transportation sector.

Career Development and Professional Growth

A career as a ride-hailing driver offers opportunities for career advancement, skill development, and professional growth within the transportation service industry. Drivers may pursue training in customer service excellence, defensive driving techniques, or vehicle operation to enhance job skills, qualify for specialized roles, or advance to supervisory positions within ride-hailing companies or transportation service providers. Professional development programs, leadership training initiatives, or continuing education opportunities enable drivers to expand career prospects, achieve career goals, and contribute to service excellence in ride-hailing transportation services.

Personal Perspectives

Ride-hailing drivers share stories of navigating city traffic, interacting with diverse passengers, and overcoming operational challenges to deliver reliable transportation services. They reflect on the satisfaction of meeting passenger needs, building customer trust, and contributing to urban mobility solutions that support ride-hailing services and meet evolving passenger travel demands in the ride-hailing transportation sector.

Chapter 27. Roadside Assistance Services

Roadside assistance service providers are essential in supporting drivers, ensuring road safety, and providing dependable help during roadside emergencies. Through their dedication to customer service excellence, safety protocols, and operational efficiency, roadside assistance professionals contribute to road safety initiatives, promote service reliability, and enhance driver confidence in accessing timely assistance in roadside assistance service operations.

Roles and Responsibilities
Roadside assistance service providers play a crucial role in offering timely support to motorists facing vehicle breakdowns, accidents, or emergencies on roads and highways. They respond to distress calls, assess vehicle issues, and provide on-the-spot repairs or towing services to ensure stranded drivers can safely resume their journeys. Roadside assistance professionals prioritize customer safety, deliver reliable assistance, and uphold service standards to alleviate stress and inconvenience for drivers experiencing roadside emergencies.

Emergency Response and Vehicle Recovery
Responding promptly to emergency calls, coordinating vehicle recovery, and providing roadside repairs are primary responsibilities for roadside assistance service providers. They deploy equipped service vehicles, assess vehicle conditions, and perform mechanical diagnostics or minor repairs to address common breakdown issues such as flat tires, battery failures, or engine malfunctions. Providers offer towing services, secure vehicles for transport, and assist drivers in accessing alternative

transportation arrangements to facilitate vehicle recovery and ensure driver safety during roadside emergencies.

Customer Service and Support

Delivering exceptional customer service, offering empathetic support, and maintaining professionalism are essential for roadside assistance professionals to enhance customer satisfaction and trust. They communicate effectively with distressed drivers, provide clear instructions or assistance updates, and offer reassurance throughout the roadside assistance process. Providers prioritize customer needs, address service inquiries, and resolve concerns promptly to foster positive customer experiences and cultivate long-term relationships in the roadside assistance service industry.

Safety Protocols and Risk Management

Adhering to safety protocols, implementing risk management strategies, and promoting driver safety are critical for roadside assistance service providers to mitigate risks, prevent accidents, and ensure personal well-being during service operations. They undergo safety training, utilize personal protective equipment, and exercise caution when working in roadside environments to minimize hazards and maintain safety standards. Providers assess traffic conditions, secure work zones, and prioritize driver safety while performing roadside assistance tasks to uphold service excellence and promote safe service delivery practices.

Vehicle Inspection and Maintenance

Conducting vehicle inspections, maintaining service vehicles, and ensuring equipment readiness are fundamental for roadside assistance professionals to support efficient service operations and deliver reliable assistance to motorists. They perform regular vehicle checks, monitor equipment functionality, and replenish supplies or tools necessary for roadside repairs or vehicle recovery efforts. Providers adhere to maintenance schedules, address equipment malfunctions promptly, and collaborate with automotive service providers to ensure operational readiness and uphold service reliability in roadside assistance operations.

Communication Technology and Dispatch Coordination

Utilizing communication technology, coordinating dispatch operations, and optimizing service response times are essential for roadside assistance service providers to deliver timely assistance and enhance operational efficiency. They use mobile dispatch systems, GPS tracking technologies, or digital communication tools to receive service requests, dispatch service vehicles, and coordinate service assignments effectively. Providers leverage real-time data updates, monitor service statuses, and communicate service progress to drivers or service recipients to facilitate seamless service delivery and ensure customer satisfaction in roadside assistance operations.

Regulatory Compliance and Service Standards

Complying with regulatory requirements, adhering to service standards, and maintaining industry certifications are priorities for roadside assistance professionals to operate legally and uphold service integrity in the roadside assistance service industry. They obtain business licenses, adhere to transportation regulations, and participate in industry training programs or certification courses to demonstrate competence and professionalism. Providers uphold ethical practices, respect customer rights, and support regulatory compliance initiatives to promote trust, accountability, and service excellence in roadside assistance service operations.

Environmental Stewardship and Sustainability

Supporting environmental stewardship, promoting sustainable practices, and reducing environmental impacts are commitments for roadside assistance service providers to contribute positively to environmental sustainability efforts. They adopt eco-friendly service practices, minimize vehicle emissions, and promote vehicle recycling or disposal solutions to reduce carbon footprints and conserve natural resources. Providers support green initiatives, implement energy-efficient technologies, and participate in environmental conservation programs to foster environmental responsibility and promote sustainable practices in roadside assistance service operations.

Crisis Management and Incident Resolution

Managing crisis situations, resolving service incidents, and ensuring effective problem-solving skills are essential for roadside assistance professionals to address complex service challenges and ensure service continuity in emergency situations. They assess service risks, implement contingency plans, and deploy resources strategically to manage service disruptions or unforeseen events affecting service delivery. Providers maintain composure, prioritize customer needs, and collaborate with emergency responders or authorities to resolve incidents promptly and restore service operations during crisis scenarios in roadside assistance services.

Community Engagement and Public Outreach

Engaging with communities, participating in public outreach initiatives, and promoting road safety awareness are initiatives for roadside assistance service providers to support community well-being and enhance public trust in roadside assistance services. They participate in community events, deliver road safety presentations, and share educational resources to promote responsible driving behaviors, emergency preparedness, and vehicle maintenance practices among motorists. Providers foster partnerships with local organizations, support charitable initiatives, and contribute to community resilience efforts to strengthen community relations and promote positive impacts in the roadside assistance service industry.

Chapter 28. School Bus Drivers

The role of a school bus driver is a responsible one, ensuring the safe transportation of students from their homes to school and back again.

Roles and Responsibilities
School bus drivers are crucial in safely transporting students to and from schools, ensuring their safety, and upholding a secure environment during transit. They adhere to strict schedules, follow designated routes, and prioritize passenger safety by enforcing safety regulations and maintaining order among students. School bus drivers conduct pre-trip inspections, monitor vehicle conditions, and communicate effectively with school administrators and parents to ensure smooth transportation operations and foster a positive educational environment for students.

Student Safety and Behavior Management
Ensuring student safety, managing student behavior, and promoting a positive atmosphere are primary responsibilities for school bus drivers. They enforce safety rules, assist students in boarding and disembarking the bus safely, and secure seat belts or safety restraints to protect passengers during travel. Drivers maintain discipline, address behavioral issues promptly, and promote respectful conduct among students to create a safe and supportive environment conducive to learning during school bus transportation.

Route Navigation and Transportation Efficiency
Navigating school routes, optimizing transportation efficiency, and adhering to transportation schedules are essential for school bus drivers to ensure punctual arrival and departure times for students.

They utilize GPS navigation systems, review route maps, and adjust travel routes based on traffic conditions or road closures to minimize delays and ensure timely transportation services for students. Drivers coordinate with school officials, communicate route updates, and maintain communication channels to facilitate efficient transportation logistics and support educational activities within school communities.

Emergency Response and Crisis Management

Responding to emergencies, managing crisis situations, and ensuring student safety during unforeseen incidents are priorities for school bus drivers to uphold safety protocols and protect student well-being in transit. They undergo emergency response training, implement evacuation procedures, and communicate effectively with emergency services or school authorities during emergencies such as accidents, severe weather conditions, or medical incidents affecting student safety. Drivers prioritize student evacuation, provide reassurance, and coordinate emergency responses to mitigate risks and ensure prompt assistance in critical situations encountered during school bus operations.

Vehicle Maintenance and Inspection

Conducting regular vehicle maintenance, performing safety inspections, and ensuring vehicle readiness are critical for school bus drivers to uphold vehicle safety standards and operational reliability in student transportation services. They inspect brake systems, check tire conditions, and monitor fluid levels to maintain optimal vehicle performance and compliance with transportation regulations. Drivers adhere to maintenance schedules, address mechanical issues promptly, and collaborate with maintenance personnel or service providers to conduct repairs and ensure safe operational conditions for school bus fleets.

Parent and Community Relations

Building positive relationships with parents, fostering community trust, and promoting open communication are integral for school bus drivers to enhance parental involvement and support student transportation needs. They engage with parents, provide transportation updates, and address parental concerns or inquiries to facilitate transparent communication and address student transportation needs effectively. Drivers collaborate with school administrators, attend parent meetings, and participate in school events to strengthen community relations, promote educational partnerships, and support student well-being through reliable school bus transportation services.

Training and Professional Development
Participating in training programs, advancing professional skills, and pursuing continuing education are priorities for school bus drivers to enhance job performance, maintain licensure requirements, and uphold industry standards in student transportation services. They undergo driver training courses, acquire commercial driver's licenses, and complete certification programs to demonstrate competence in operating school buses and ensuring passenger safety. Drivers engage in professional development opportunities, attend workshops, and stay informed about transportation regulations or safety protocols to enhance operational knowledge and skills necessary for effective school bus transportation services.

Educational Support and Student Engagement
Supporting educational initiatives, promoting student engagement, and fostering a positive learning environment are commitments for school bus drivers to contribute to academic success and student development during school bus transportation. They encourage student participation in educational activities, provide assistance with educational materials, and promote positive interactions among students to enhance educational experiences and support student learning during school bus travel. Drivers collaborate with

educators, reinforce classroom lessons, and promote student safety to facilitate a conducive learning environment and contribute to student achievement through reliable school bus transportation services.

Community Outreach and Safety Advocacy
Engaging in community outreach, advocating for safety initiatives, and promoting road safety awareness are initiatives for school bus drivers to support community well-being and enhance public awareness of student transportation safety. They participate in safety campaigns, deliver presentations on bus safety rules, and educate students about safe behaviors during school bus travel to promote responsible road safety practices among young passengers. Drivers collaborate with local organizations, support safety initiatives, and contribute to community resilience efforts to strengthen community relations and promote positive impacts in student transportation services.

Reflections on Service and Impact
Reflecting on service experiences, celebrating milestones, and acknowledging the impact of school bus transportation on student lives inspire school bus drivers in their commitment to providing reliable transportation services and ensuring student well-being. They cherish moments of student gratitude, celebrate achievements, and recognize the role of school bus transportation in supporting educational opportunities and promoting student success within school communities. Drivers embrace the responsibility, honor student trust, and take pride in their contributions to student transportation safety, educational support, and community engagement through dedicated service in school bus transportation roles.

Chapter 29. Sightseeing Tour Bus Drivers

The role of sightseeing tour bus drivers is fascinating as they take tourists daily to explore and showcase the beauty around. This job entails significant responsibilities and unique challenges while ensuring memorable experiences for passengers.

Roles and Responsibilities

Sightseeing tour bus drivers play a crucial role in providing informative and enjoyable tours for passengers visiting various attractions and landmarks. They operate large tour buses, follow designated routes, and narrate engaging commentary about historical sites, cultural landmarks, and points of interest to enhance the sightseeing experience. Tour bus drivers prioritize passenger safety, maintain vehicle cleanliness, and ensure adherence to tour schedules to deliver memorable and educational sightseeing tours for tourists and travelers.

Narration and Tour Commentary

Delivering informative narration, providing insightful tour commentary, and engaging passengers in cultural and historical insights are the primary responsibilities of sightseeing tour bus drivers. They share knowledge about local landmarks, historical events, and cultural traditions to enrich passenger understanding and appreciation of sightseeing destinations. Drivers deliver commentary in multiple languages, tailor information to passenger interests, and interact with passengers to create interactive and educational sightseeing experiences that highlight the uniqueness and significance of each tour destination.

Route Navigation and Tour Logistics

Navigating tour routes, optimizing tour logistics, and ensuring timely arrivals at designated stops are essential for sightseeing tour bus drivers to facilitate smooth tour operations and maximize passenger satisfaction. They review tour itineraries, coordinate with tour operators, and adjust routes based on traffic conditions or tour schedule changes to maintain tour efficiency and meet passenger expectations. Drivers utilize GPS navigation systems, consult route maps, and communicate with tour guides to ensure seamless tour logistics and enhance the overall sightseeing experience for passengers.

Customer Service and Passenger Engagement
Providing exceptional customer service, fostering positive passenger interactions, and ensuring passenger comfort are priorities for sightseeing tour bus drivers to enhance passenger satisfaction and enjoyment during sightseeing tours. They greet passengers warmly, assist with boarding and disembarking, and address passenger inquiries or special requests promptly to create a welcoming and accommodating atmosphere onboard tour buses. Drivers engage with passengers, encourage interaction, and promote a friendly and informative environment to enrich passenger experiences and foster memorable sightseeing tour moments for tourists and travelers.

Vehicle Maintenance and Safety Checks
Conducting routine vehicle maintenance, performing pre-trip safety checks, and ensuring vehicle reliability are critical for sightseeing tour bus drivers to uphold safety standards and operational efficiency in tour transportation services. They inspect bus systems, monitor mechanical components, and verify emergency equipment to maintain safe operating conditions and comply with transportation regulations. Drivers adhere to maintenance schedules, address vehicle issues promptly, and collaborate with maintenance personnel to ensure reliable tour bus performance and passenger safety throughout sightseeing tours.

Cultural Sensitivity and Tour Interpretation

Demonstrating cultural sensitivity, providing accurate tour interpretation, and respecting local customs are essential for sightseeing tour bus drivers to promote cultural awareness and appreciation among passengers during sightseeing tours. They share insights into cultural practices, historical significance, and local traditions associated with tour destinations to enhance passenger understanding and cultural immersion experiences. Drivers facilitate respectful interactions, uphold cultural sensitivity guidelines, and promote cross-cultural exchange to foster meaningful connections and enrich sightseeing tour experiences for diverse passenger groups.

Tourist Assistance and Local Knowledge

Offering tourist assistance, sharing local knowledge, and providing recommendations for dining, shopping, or additional attractions are initiatives for sightseeing tour bus drivers to support passenger enjoyment and facilitate memorable travel experiences. They offer tips on popular tourist spots, suggest dining options, and provide insights into local entertainment venues or recreational activities to enhance passenger exploration and enjoyment of tour destinations. Drivers serve as local ambassadors, offer insider perspectives, and contribute to tourist satisfaction by sharing personalized recommendations and local insights during sightseeing tours.

Environmental Awareness and Sustainable Tourism

Promoting environmental awareness, advocating for sustainable tourism practices, and minimizing environmental impacts are commitments for sightseeing tour bus drivers to support eco-friendly tour operations and preserve natural resources in tour destinations. They promote responsible tourism behaviors, encourage waste reduction initiatives, and adhere to eco-friendly guidelines to minimize carbon footprints and conserve natural habitats during sightseeing tours. Drivers support sustainable tourism initiatives, participate in environmental conservation efforts, and educate passengers on eco-friendly travel practices to promote environmental stewardship and contribute positively to sustainable tourism initiatives in sightseeing tour operations.

Professional Development and Tour Enhancement

Participating in professional development opportunities, advancing tour management skills, and pursuing continuous learning are priorities for sightseeing tour bus drivers to enhance tour quality and customer satisfaction in sightseeing tour services. They undergo tour guide training, acquire cultural knowledge, and refine communication skills to deliver informative and engaging sightseeing experiences for passengers. Drivers engage in industry workshops, attend tourism seminars, and embrace technological advancements to incorporate multimedia tools or interactive features that enhance tour narration and elevate the overall sightseeing tour experience for tourists and travelers.

Reflections on Tour Impact and Passenger Experiences

Reflecting on tour impact, celebrating positive passenger feedback, and acknowledging the influence of sightseeing tours on passenger experiences inspire sightseeing tour bus drivers in their commitment to delivering exceptional tour services and fostering cultural appreciation. They value passenger testimonials, embrace moments of passenger appreciation, and recognize the significance of sightseeing tours in promoting travel exploration, cultural understanding, and memorable experiences for tourists and travelers. Drivers take pride in their role as tour guides, share in passenger enjoyment, and contribute to the success of sightseeing tours by delivering enriching and transformative travel experiences through dedicated service in sightseeing tour bus driver roles.

Chapter 30. Taxi Drivers

Taxi drivers play a vital role in urban transportation, providing essential services that connect passengers to their destinations safely and efficiently. They uphold high standards of customer service, adhere to regulatory requirements, and adapt to changes in the transportation landscape to meet the diverse needs of passengers and communities. Taxi drivers contribute significantly to city dynamics, support local economies, and play an integral part in enhancing urban mobility and accessibility for residents and visitors alike.

Roles and Responsibilities
Taxi drivers assume a pivotal role in urban transportation, offering essential on-demand services to passengers. They are tasked with safely navigating city streets, efficiently picking up passengers from designated locations, and transporting them to their destinations promptly. Drivers must maintain their vehicles in optimal condition, ensuring cleanliness and mechanical reliability to uphold passenger comfort and safety standards. Additionally, they adhere strictly to traffic laws and regulations while providing courteous and professional service to passengers.

Customer Service and Communication
Exceptional customer service is paramount for taxi drivers, as they interact directly with passengers throughout their journeys. They greet passengers warmly, assist with luggage as needed, and maintain a friendly demeanor to enhance the overall experience. Effective communication skills are crucial for addressing passenger inquiries, providing route suggestions, and ensuring passengers feel comfortable during the ride. Moreover, drivers handle payment transactions efficiently, issue receipts promptly, and address any concerns or special requests from passengers to ensure satisfaction and build customer loyalty.

Route Navigation and Efficiency

Navigating city routes efficiently is a critical skill for taxi drivers to minimize travel time and maximize passenger convenience. They utilize GPS navigation systems and local knowledge to select the most efficient routes, considering factors such as traffic conditions and road closures. Taxi drivers stay informed about alternative routes and transportation updates to adapt quickly to changing traffic patterns and provide smooth transportation services. Efficiency in route navigation not only enhances passenger satisfaction but also optimizes driver earnings by reducing idle time and maximizing the number of fares per shift.

Safety and Vehicle Maintenance

Ensuring passenger safety is a top priority for taxi drivers, who conduct regular inspections and maintenance checks on their vehicles. They inspect brakes, tires, lights, and other essential components to maintain vehicle reliability and comply with safety standards. Drivers are trained to handle emergency situations effectively, such as accidents or mechanical failures, to ensure the safety and well-being of passengers. Moreover, they enforce seat belt usage and adhere to traffic regulations to mitigate risks and provide a secure travel environment for passengers.

Financial Management and Regulations

Effective financial management is crucial for taxi drivers to maintain their business operations and achieve profitability. They adhere to local fare regulations, prominently display fare information in their vehicles, and issue accurate receipts for all transactions. Taxi drivers maintain detailed records of daily earnings, expenses, and operational costs related to fuel, maintenance, and vehicle lease or ownership. They strive to optimize their earnings by strategically planning shifts, monitoring demand patterns, and adapting to fluctuations in passenger demand during peak hours or seasons.

Challenges and Adaptability
Taxi drivers face various challenges in their profession, including competition from ride-sharing services, fluctuating demand, and regulatory changes impacting fare structures or operating conditions. They must adapt to technological advancements in transportation, such as mobile apps for dispatch and customer bookings, to remain competitive in the market. Additionally, drivers navigate challenges related to customer preferences, traffic congestion, and unpredictable weather conditions that affect travel times and service availability. Adaptability is crucial for taxi drivers to innovate service offerings, improve customer satisfaction, and sustain their livelihoods amidst evolving industry trends.

Community Engagement and Reputation
Building a positive reputation within the community enhances the credibility and trustworthiness of taxi drivers among passengers and local businesses. They participate in community events, support initiatives that benefit residents, and foster positive relationships with passengers through exemplary service. Taxi drivers prioritize passenger feedback, address concerns promptly, and maintain professionalism to cultivate long-term customer relationships and foster loyalty. A strong reputation contributes to business sustainability and strengthens their role as integral contributors to urban mobility and transportation services.

Future Outlook and Sustainability
Looking ahead, taxi drivers anticipate advancements in electric vehicles, autonomous driving technology, and sustainable transportation solutions. They explore opportunities to integrate eco-friendly vehicles into their fleets, participate in training programs on new technologies, and advocate for policies promoting environmental sustainability in urban transportation. Taxi drivers play a pivotal role in shaping the future of urban mobility by embracing innovation, supporting sustainable

development goals, and contributing to efforts aimed at reducing carbon emissions and improving air quality in cities.

Chapter 31. Tow Truck Operators

Tow truck operators are crucial in promoting road safety, delivering essential roadside assistance services, and contributing to community well-being. They exemplify professionalism, expertise in vehicle recovery, and commitment to public safety through rigorous training, adherence to regulatory standards, and proactive maintenance practices. Tow truck operators are indispensable partners in urban mobility, offering reliable assistance and peace of mind to motorists during roadside emergencies.

Roles and Responsibilities
Tow truck operators are essential for ensuring the smooth flow of traffic and responding promptly to roadside emergencies. They play a critical role in towing vehicles that are disabled, illegally parked, or involved in accidents. Operators must efficiently secure vehicles using specialized equipment such as chains, straps, or wheel lifts, ensuring they are transported safely to designated locations or repair facilities. Furthermore, operators must comply with local regulations and safety standards to prevent vehicle damage and uphold public safety.

Emergency Response and Safety
Operating under urgent and sometimes hazardous conditions, tow truck operators prioritize safety protocols to protect themselves, motorists, and bystanders. They assess potential risks at accident scenes, deploy safety cones and warning lights, and communicate effectively with law enforcement and emergency personnel to coordinate response efforts. Operators undergo rigorous training in vehicle recovery techniques and first-aid procedures to handle diverse roadside emergencies with professionalism and efficiency.

Vehicle Recovery Techniques

Tow truck operators employ a variety of specialized techniques to recover vehicles from challenging situations. Whether extracting cars from ditches, off-road locations, or accident scenes, operators utilize winches, hydraulic lifts, and other heavy-duty equipment to safely maneuver vehicles onto their trucks. Each recovery operation requires precision and skill to minimize further damage to vehicles and ensure they are transported securely to repair facilities or designated impound lots.

Customer Service and Communication

Exceptional customer service is integral to the role of tow truck operators, who often assist distressed vehicle owners during stressful situations. They approach each interaction with empathy and professionalism, offering clear explanations of towing procedures, estimated timelines, and costs involved. Operators prioritize customer satisfaction by providing assistance with alternative transportation arrangements, recommending reputable repair shops, and offering reassurance to alleviate concerns.

Regulatory Compliance and Documentation

Adherence to regulatory requirements is paramount for tow truck operators to operate legally and ethically. They maintain meticulous records of towed vehicles, complete necessary paperwork for vehicle impoundment or storage, and ensure compliance with local towing ordinances and insurance regulations. Operators uphold transparency in pricing, display fee schedules prominently in their vehicles, and issue detailed receipts for all services rendered to maintain trust and accountability with customers.

Challenges and Hazards

Tow truck operators face numerous challenges in their profession, including heavy traffic, adverse weather conditions, and the risk of encountering impaired or distracted drivers at accident scenes.

They must remain vigilant and adaptable, employing defensive driving techniques and situational awareness to mitigate risks and ensure personal safety while performing roadside assistance duties. Operators undergo continuous training to enhance their skills in hazard recognition, emergency response, and conflict resolution to navigate unpredictable roadside environments effectively.

Vehicle Maintenance and Equipment
Maintaining tow trucks and equipment in optimal condition is essential for operational reliability and customer satisfaction. Tow truck operators conduct routine inspections, perform preventive maintenance tasks, and address mechanical issues promptly to minimize downtime and ensure readiness for emergency responses. They invest in state-of-the-art equipment upgrades, such as GPS navigation systems and digital dispatch technology, to streamline operations, improve route efficiency, and enhance overall service delivery capabilities.

Industry Trends and Technology
Technological advancements are pivotal in reshaping the towing industry. Tow truck operators embrace digital dispatch systems, mobile applications for real-time updates, and GPS tracking to optimize fleet management and improve response times. They leverage technology to enhance customer communication, provide accurate service estimates, and maintain operational transparency. Operators stay informed about emerging trends in electric and autonomous vehicles, exploring opportunities to incorporate eco-friendly practices and sustainable solutions into their towing operations.

Community Engagement and Professionalism
Building trust and credibility within the community is fundamental for tow truck operators. They actively participate in community events, support local initiatives, and demonstrate professionalism

in all interactions with customers and stakeholders. Operators prioritize ethical conduct, resolve conflicts diplomatically, and uphold a positive reputation for reliability and integrity in delivering roadside assistance services. By fostering strong relationships and maintaining high standards of service excellence, tow truck operators contribute to community resilience and enhance public perception of the towing profession.

Future Outlook and Sustainability
Looking ahead, tow truck operators anticipate ongoing advancements in vehicle technology, environmental regulations, and industry standards. They embrace opportunities for professional development, such as training in hybrid and electric vehicle recovery techniques, to adapt to evolving customer needs and market demands. Tow truck operators advocate for sustainable practices in vehicle disposal and recycling, promoting environmental stewardship, and supporting initiatives that reduce carbon emissions and preserve natural resources. As integral contributors to road safety and transportation efficiency, tow truck operators continue to play a pivotal role in shaping the future of urban mobility and sustainable towing solutions.

Chapter 32. Train Drivers

Train drivers, also known as locomotive engineers, play a pivotal role in the transportation industry by operating trains safely and efficiently across railways. Their responsibilities include ensuring the smooth movement of passengers and freight and adhering to strict schedules and safety protocols. Integral to the efficient operation of railway networks, they combine technical expertise, safety awareness, and operational proficiency to transport goods and passengers across vast distances. Their commitment to safety and dedication to service excellence ensure the reliability and sustainability of rail transportation systems, contributing significantly to transportation infrastructure and community connectivity.

Roles and Responsibilities
Train drivers are tasked with operating locomotives to transport passengers or freight according to established timetables and routes. They start by inspecting their locomotives and performing safety checks to ensure mechanical reliability. During the journey, drivers monitor gauges, signals, and track conditions, adjusting speed and applying brakes as necessary to maintain safety and efficiency. They communicate with dispatchers and railway personnel to coordinate movements and respond to unexpected situations such as track obstructions or mechanical failures.

Safety and Compliance
Safety is paramount for train drivers, who must comply with stringent regulations and protocols to protect passengers, crew, and cargo. They receive thorough training in operational procedures, emergency protocols, and equipment usage to effectively manage diverse scenarios. Drivers enforce safety measures such as speed limits, signal adherence, and proper

braking techniques to prevent accidents and ensure the integrity of railway operations.

Route Familiarity and Navigation
Train drivers develop in-depth knowledge of railway routes, including track layouts, gradients, and station locations. They utilize this familiarity to navigate effectively, optimizing travel times and ensuring punctuality. Drivers may encounter challenges, such as adverse weather conditions or maintenance work, that require them to adjust their approach while maintaining operational efficiency and passenger comfort.

Technical Expertise and Maintenance
Beyond operating trains, drivers possess technical expertise in locomotive systems and equipment. They monitor engine performance, fuel consumption, and mechanical components to identify potential issues and perform minor repairs or adjustments as needed. Regular maintenance tasks, such as lubrication, cleaning, and inspections, are essential to keep locomotives in optimal condition and prevent operational disruptions.

Communication and Coordination
Effective communication is critical for train drivers, who maintain contact with dispatchers, signal operators, and onboard crew members throughout their journeys. They relay important information, such as track conditions, signal changes, and schedule updates, to ensure smooth coordination and safe passage. Drivers collaborate closely with railway personnel to resolve operational issues promptly and maintain seamless operations across the rail network.

Challenges and Adaptability
Train drivers face challenges unique to rail transportation, including navigating complex rail networks, managing heavy cargo loads, and responding to unpredictable weather conditions. They

must remain adaptable, making quick decisions in dynamic environments while prioritizing safety and regulatory compliance. Drivers undergo continuous training to stay current with industry advancements, safety regulations, and technological innovations that enhance operational efficiency and safety.

Career Development and Opportunities

A career as a train driver offers opportunities for professional growth and advancement within the railway industry. Drivers may specialize in specific types of trains, such as passenger or freight services, or pursue roles in training new recruits or advancing to supervisory positions. Continuing education and certification programs enable drivers to enhance their skills, qualify for higher-level responsibilities, and contribute to the evolving landscape of rail transportation.

Community Impact and Responsibility

Train drivers play a vital role in supporting regional economies and connecting communities through reliable transportation services. They uphold public trust by delivering passengers and freight safely, contributing to economic development, and reducing road congestion and environmental impact. Drivers engage with local communities, participate in railway safety initiatives, and promote public awareness of rail transportation's benefits and contributions to sustainable mobility.

Chapter 33. Tram Drivers

Tram drivers demonstrate professionalism and dedication as they contribute significantly to urban mobility. Their responsibilities include safe tram operation, passenger care, environmental stewardship, and community engagement. By upholding the integrity of public transport systems, tram drivers support sustainable urban development and improve the quality of life for city residents and visitors. They play a pivotal role in urban transportation systems, navigating bustling city streets and suburban areas with precision and responsibility. Operating trams not only enhances public transport efficiency but also enhances the aesthetic appeal and ecological benefits of urban mobility.

Responsibilities and Duties
Tram drivers are entrusted with the safe and reliable operation of trams, ensuring passengers reach their destinations on time and in comfort. They adhere to strict schedules, manage ticketing and fare collection, and maintain courteous interactions with passengers. Additionally, tram drivers oversee the boarding and disembarking process, ensuring the efficient flow of passengers at each stop.

Driving in Urban Environments
Driving a tram in a crowded city requires exceptional skill and awareness. Tram drivers must navigate through dense traffic, pedestrian crossings, and narrow streets while adhering to traffic signals and safety protocols. They prioritize pedestrian safety by maintaining cautious speeds and adhering to designated tram tracks to prevent accidents and ensure smooth transit operations.

Ecological Impact
Trams are recognized for their environmental benefits, as they contribute to reducing carbon emissions and traffic congestion in

urban areas. Tram drivers play a crucial role in promoting sustainable transportation solutions by encouraging public transit use and reducing reliance on individual vehicles. Their commitment to eco-friendly practices supports broader efforts towards urban sustainability and cleaner air quality.

Vehicle Maintenance and Safety Checks

Ensuring the safety and reliability of trams is a primary responsibility for tram drivers. They conduct thorough pre-departure inspections, checking tram systems, brakes, doors, and emergency equipment. Tram drivers promptly report any maintenance issues to maintenance staff and collaborate closely to address and resolve technical concerns, ensuring passenger safety and operational efficiency.

Community Engagement

Tram drivers engage with the community by participating in public events, promoting tram services, and fostering positive relationships with passengers. They provide informative commentary on local landmarks, historical sites, and points of interest during tram journeys, enhancing the overall passenger experience. Tram drivers contribute to the cultural and social fabric of cities, connecting residents and visitors through reliable and accessible public transport services.

Professional Development

Continuous professional development is essential for tram drivers to maintain high standards of service and safety. They participate in ongoing training programs on tram operations, emergency response procedures, customer service, and new technology integration. Tram drivers strive for proficiency in tram handling techniques and safety protocols, ensuring they deliver exemplary service to passengers while advancing their careers in urban transportation.

Chapter 34. Truck (Lorry) Drivers

Truck driving stands as a cornerstone of global logistics, encompassing a profession that spans continents, delivers essential goods, and fuels economic growth. At its core, being a truck driver is about more than navigating highways and delivering cargo—it's a lifestyle that demands resilience, skill, and a deep commitment to safety and efficiency. From the moment drivers conduct their pre-trip inspections to the hours spent on the road, they embody the essence of reliability and professionalism. This chapter explores the intricate web of responsibilities, challenges, and unique aspects of life on the road for truck drivers, shedding light on their pivotal role in keeping supply chains moving and economies thriving worldwide.

Responsibilities and Duties
Truck drivers shoulder the critical responsibility of transporting goods across extensive distances, ensuring timely deliveries, and maintaining supply chain efficiency. Their duties begin with thorough pre-trip inspections to verify vehicle safety and compliance with regulatory standards. Throughout their journeys, drivers must secure and protect cargo, navigate diverse road conditions, and adhere to traffic laws to ensure the safe and efficient movement of goods.

Types of Trucks and Trailers
Truck drivers operate a variety of vehicles tailored to specific cargo needs. This includes standard tractor-trailers, flatbeds for transporting oversized loads, refrigerated trucks for perishable goods, and tankers for liquid cargo. Each type of truck requires specialized handling skills and knowledge to ensure safe operation and secure transportation of diverse commodities.

Licensing and Training Requirements

Obtaining a commercial driver's license (CDL) is a foundational requirement for truck drivers, with specific endorsements needed for different types of vehicles and cargo. Training programs encompass both classroom instruction and practical experience, covering topics such as vehicle operation, defensive driving techniques, and regulatory compliance. Ongoing education ensures drivers stay abreast of industry standards and safety protocols.

Safety Regulations and Compliance

Truck drivers adhere to stringent safety regulations to protect themselves, their cargo, and other road users. This includes regular vehicle inspections, compliance with weight limits, and adherence to hours-of-service regulations to prevent driver fatigue. Drivers prioritize safety protocols to mitigate risks and ensure compliance with local, state, and federal transportation laws.

Route Planning and Navigation

Effective route planning is essential for optimizing travel times and fuel efficiency. Truck drivers utilize advanced GPS navigation systems and traditional maps to plan routes that minimize congestion, road construction, and other potential delays. Strategic planning ensures timely deliveries while adhering to customer schedules and maximizing operational efficiency.

Vehicle Inspections and Maintenance

Maintaining mechanical reliability is paramount for truck drivers. They conduct thorough pre-trip inspections to check brakes, tires, lights, and other essential components. Regular maintenance and timely repairs prevent breakdowns, reduce downtime, and enhance overall vehicle performance. Drivers prioritize proactive maintenance to ensure safety, operational efficiency, and regulatory compliance.

Cargo Loading and Securing

Ensuring cargo is properly loaded and securely fastened is crucial to prevent shifting or damage during transportation. Truck drivers utilize equipment such as straps, chains, and load bars to secure loads according to safety standards. They carefully distribute cargo to maintain vehicle stability and adhere to weight distribution regulations. Effective cargo management reduces risks and ensures the safe transport of goods.

Driving Techniques and Skills

Truck drivers have developed advanced driving skills through extensive experience and training. They maneuver large vehicles, execute precise backing maneuvers, and navigate through challenging terrain and weather conditions. Defensive driving techniques enable drivers to anticipate potential hazards, respond to emergencies, and prioritize safety while maintaining operational efficiency.

Challenges on the Road

Truck drivers encounter a multitude of challenges while on the road, necessitating resilience and adaptability. Truck drivers face the challenge of navigating through adverse weather conditions like rain, snow, and fog, which can greatly affect visibility and road conditions. Heavy traffic, road closures, and construction zones necessitate strategic navigation and proactive planning to minimize delays and ensure on-time deliveries.

Long Hours and Fatigue Management

Truck drivers manage demanding schedules that often involve long hours behind the wheel. To combat driver fatigue and prioritize safety, truck drivers adhere to hours-of-service regulations stipulating maximum driving times and mandatory rest periods. Drivers prioritize sufficient sleep, healthy eating habits, and regular exercise to maintain physical and mental well-being during extended periods on the road.

Lifestyle on the Road

Truck drivers adjust to a distinctive lifestyle that includes prolonged periods away from home. They live in their trucks, equipped with sleeping berths, cooking facilities, and basic amenities for personal hygiene. Drivers embrace self-sufficiency, managing daily routines while navigating the challenges of isolation and limited social interaction. Communication technologies enable drivers to stay connected with family and loved ones while fulfilling their professional responsibilities.

Communication and Logistics Coordination

Effective communication is essential for truck drivers to coordinate pick-ups and deliveries and resolve logistical challenges. They maintain regular contact with dispatchers, shippers, and receivers using mobile phones and communication systems. Clear communication ensures seamless operations, enhances customer satisfaction, and resolves issues promptly to maintain supply chain efficiency.

Technology and Tools Used

Truck drivers leverage technology to enhance operational efficiency and safety during their journeys. GPS navigation systems provide real-time route guidance, optimizing travel routes and minimizing fuel consumption. Electronic Logging Devices (ELDs) track hours of service, ensuring compliance with regulatory limits and promoting driver safety. Telematics systems monitor vehicle performance metrics, allowing for proactive maintenance and reducing downtime.

Health and Well-Being Considerations

Prioritizing physical and mental health is crucial for truck drivers who navigate the challenges of sedentary work and irregular schedules. They prioritize healthy eating habits, regular exercise, and sufficient sleep to mitigate the health risks associated with long hours of driving. Drivers adopt strategies for stress management, mindfulness, and maintaining positive mental health to enhance overall well-being.

Time Away from Home and Family

Truck drivers navigate prolonged absences from home while juggling their professional duties and personal obligations. Companies may offer flexible scheduling options or designated home time to support drivers' emotional well-being and maintain work-life balance. Drivers utilize communication technologies to stay connected with family and loved ones, fostering relationships despite geographical distance.

Eating and Cooking Arrangements

Truck drivers adapt to diverse dining options while on the road, including cooking meals in their trucks and patronizing truck stops and restaurants along their routes. They prioritize nutrition and meal planning to maintain health and well-being during extended periods away from home. Drivers may carry portable cooking appliances and food supplies to prepare meals that meet dietary preferences and nutritional needs.

Financial Considerations

Truck drivers' earnings fluctuate depending on their experience level, the type of cargo they transport, and the demand within the industry. They incur expenses for fuel, maintenance, meals, and accommodations, which impact their overall earnings and financial stability. Drivers manage financial resources through budgeting and expense tracking to optimize earnings and maintain economic stability within the trucking industry.

Environmental Impact and Sustainability Efforts

Truck drivers are increasingly mindful of their environmental footprint and adopt practices to reduce emissions and conserve resources. They participate in sustainable transportation initiatives by optimizing fuel efficiency, reducing idle times, and supporting the use of alternative energy sources such as biodiesel fuels. Drivers advocate for environmental stewardship through efficient route planning and vehicle maintenance practices that contribute to air quality improvement and resource conservation.

Economic Contribution to Supply Chains

Truck drivers play a pivotal role in global supply chains by facilitating the timely and reliable delivery of goods essential to industries and consumers worldwide. Their efficiency in transporting raw materials, finished products, and perishable goods supports supply chain operations, maintains inventory levels, and meets consumer demand. Drivers' contributions to logistics and distribution contribute to economic growth, stability, and international trade.

Career Opportunities and Advancement

Truck driving offers diverse career opportunities for advancement and specialization within the industry. Drivers may pursue specialized roles such as tanker or hazmat drivers, fleet managers, or owner-operators. Continuing education and certifications enhance professional development, expand job prospects, and increase earning potential within the competitive trucking sector.

Community and Social Aspects

Truck drivers form a close-knit community, sharing experiences, insights, and support through industry associations, online forums, and social media platforms. They contribute to local economies by patronizing truck stops, restaurants, and businesses along their routes. Drivers foster camaraderie and solidarity through mutual respect and understanding, creating a supportive network within the trucking profession.

Regulatory Changes and Industry Trends

Staying informed about regulatory changes, technological advancements, and industry trends is essential for truck drivers to maintain compliance and adapt to evolving standards in transportation and logistics. Drivers undergo ongoing training and education to stay abreast of regulatory requirements, safety protocols, and best practices that enhance operational efficiency and professionalism within the trucking industry.

Chapter 35. Valet Drivers

Valet drivers are responsible for efficiently managing parking spaces to ensure convenience for drivers, providing safe and satisfactory parking solutions for customers' vehicles.

Responsibilities and Duties
Valet drivers are entrusted with the responsibility of providing seamless parking services for guests at hotels, restaurants, and events. Beyond simply parking cars, they ensure each vehicle is parked safely and securely in designated areas. Valet drivers meticulously inspect vehicles for any pre-existing damage and document details to maintain transparency and accountability. They handle guests' keys with care and adhere to strict protocols to safeguard against any mishandling or unauthorized access.

Customer Service Excellence
Exceptional customer service is at the heart of a valet driver's role. They greet guests warmly upon arrival, offering a welcoming and professional demeanor. Valet drivers assist guests with luggage and provide directions or recommendations as needed. Their goal is to create a positive first impression and leave guests feeling well cared for throughout their visit. They maintain open communication to address any concerns promptly and ensure a smooth parking experience.

Vehicle Handling and Maneuvering
Valet drivers demonstrate advanced driving skills to maneuver a wide range of vehicles in various parking scenarios. From compact cars to luxury SUVs, they navigate tight spaces and busy parking lots with precision and caution. Valet drivers prioritize safety at all times, employing defensive driving techniques and awareness of their surroundings to prevent accidents and ensure the smooth flow of traffic.

Safety and Security Protocols

Ensuring the safety and security of guests' vehicles is a top priority for valet drivers. Before parking a vehicle, they conduct thorough inspections to note any existing damage and verify the functionality of lights, brakes, and other essential features. Valet drivers implement stringent key management practices to prevent unauthorized access and maintain the integrity of each vehicle in their care. They adhere to established procedures to mitigate risks and uphold the trust of both guests and employers.

Fast-Paced Environments

Working in dynamic and fast-paced environments, valet drivers must perform their duties efficiently and with a sense of urgency. They handle multiple vehicles simultaneously during peak times, prioritizing incoming requests and managing parking logistics effectively. Valet drivers maintain order in the parking area, ensuring vehicles are parked in an organized manner to maximize space and accessibility for guests.

Professionalism and Presentation

Valet drivers embody professionalism in their appearance and conduct, reflecting the standards of the establishments they represent. They wear designated uniforms that are clean, well-maintained, and presentable. Valet drivers maintain cleanliness in both the vehicles they park and the parking area itself, creating a welcoming and orderly environment for guests. Their courteous and respectful demeanor enhances the overall guest experience and contributes to a positive reputation for the establishment.

Communication Skills

Effective communication is essential for valet drivers to interact with guests, colleagues, and management seamlessly. They provide clear instructions to guests regarding parking procedures, anticipated wait times, and retrieval processes. Valet drivers communicate any delays or issues promptly, ensuring guests are informed and their expectations are managed effectively. They also collaborate with team members to coordinate parking operations and resolve challenges as they arise.

Problem-Solving Abilities

Valet drivers demonstrate quick thinking and adaptability to navigate unexpected challenges in their role. They may encounter issues such as vehicle malfunctions, inclement weather conditions, or congested parking areas. Valet drivers remain calm under pressure, assess situations promptly, and implement solutions to minimize disruptions and uphold service standards. Their proactive approach ensures guest satisfaction and operational efficiency throughout their shift.

Time Management

Efficient time management is crucial for valet drivers to fulfill guest requests promptly and maintain smooth parking operations. They prioritize tasks based on urgency and guest arrival times, optimizing parking arrangements to accommodate fluctuating demand. Valet drivers coordinate vehicle retrieval efficiently to minimize wait times for guests, demonstrating attentiveness to service details and commitment to enhancing overall guest satisfaction.

Team Collaboration

Valet drivers often work as part of a collaborative team, supporting one another to deliver exceptional parking services. They communicate effectively with colleagues to coordinate vehicle movements, share workload responsibilities, and maintain consistent service standards. Valet drivers foster a supportive work environment by assisting teammates during busy periods and contributing to a cohesive team dynamic that enhances operational efficiency and guest satisfaction.

Continuous Improvement

Valet drivers engage in ongoing training and professional development to enhance their skills and stay up-to-date on industry trends. They participate in workshops, safety seminars, and customer service training programs to refine their knowledge and proficiency. Valet drivers embrace opportunities for growth and apply new insights to deliver superior parking services, reinforcing their commitment to excellence and continuous improvement in their role.

Guest Satisfaction

Ultimately, valet drivers strive to exceed guest expectations and leave a positive impression through their attentive service and professionalism. They contribute to the overall guest experience by providing seamless parking solutions, personalized assistance, and a welcoming atmosphere. Valet drivers play a pivotal role in enhancing guest satisfaction and loyalty, reflecting the establishment's commitment to hospitality and exceptional service delivery.

Chapter 36. Watercraft Drivers

Watercraft drivers play a vital role in maritime transportation, tourism, and environmental conservation efforts. They uphold safety standards, navigate complex waterways, and ensure a memorable experience for passengers. This chapter explores the diverse responsibilities and challenges faced by watercraft drivers, highlighting their contributions to marine operations and the broader maritime industry.

Responsibilities and Duties

Watercraft drivers are responsible for operating various types of water vessels, including boats, ships, ferries, and yachts. Their primary duties involve navigating waterways safely and efficiently, adhering to maritime regulations, and ensuring the safety of passengers and cargo. They may also be responsible for maintenance checks, emergency procedures, and communicating with port authorities.

Skills and Qualifications

Successful watercraft drivers possess a combination of technical skills and maritime knowledge. They must be proficient in navigation techniques, understanding water currents, tides, and weather conditions. Communication skills are essential for interacting with crew members, passengers, and authorities, while problem-solving abilities are crucial for handling emergencies at sea.

Safety Protocols

Watercraft drivers prioritize safety above all else. They conduct thorough safety checks before departure, ensure all safety equipment is onboard and in working condition, and implement emergency protocols as needed. They must be prepared to respond quickly and effectively to accidents, medical emergencies, or adverse weather conditions that may arise during voyages.

Environmental Awareness

Watercraft drivers are often stewards of the marine environment. They adhere to environmental regulations to minimize their vessel's impact on marine ecosystems, such as reducing emissions, preventing oil spills, and respecting wildlife habitats. They may participate in conservation efforts and educate passengers on responsible boating practices.

Passenger and Cargo Handling

Depending on the type of vessel, watercraft drivers may be responsible for loading and unloading passengers and cargo safely. They ensure proper weight distribution and balance to uphold stability and prevent accidents. They provide clear instructions to passengers on safety procedures and emergency exits, fostering a secure and comfortable onboard experience.

Maintenance and Inspections

Regular upkeep of watercraft is vital for maintaining operational efficiency and ensuring safety standards are met. Drivers oversee routine inspections, maintenance checks, and repairs of engines, navigational equipment, and safety systems. They keep thorough documentation of maintenance tasks and work closely with marine engineers and technicians to swiftly resolve any issues that arise.

Regulatory Compliance

Watercraft drivers must adhere to local, national, and international maritime regulations governing vessel operations, safety standards, and environmental protection. They stay informed about regulatory changes and undergo training to maintain compliance with licensing requirements and certifications.

Navigation and Maneuvering

Operating a watercraft requires expert navigation skills to navigate through varying water conditions, congested waterways, and busy harbors. Drivers use navigational tools, charts, and radar systems to plot courses, avoid obstacles, and ensure efficient routes. They adapt their navigation strategies based on weather forecasts and maritime traffic patterns.

Emergency Response

Watercraft operators undergo rigorous training to promptly and effectively respond to emergencies. They conduct drills with crew members to practice emergency procedures, such as man-overboard situations, fire emergencies, and abandoning ship protocols. They coordinate with emergency services and authorities during crisis situations to ensure the safety of all onboard.

Cultural and Tourism Roles

In addition to transportation and cargo operations, watercraft drivers may play a role in cultural tourism and recreational activities. They provide guided tours, historical insights, and information about local landmarks and attractions to enhance passengers' experiences. They promote tourism destinations and contribute to the local economy through marine tourism initiatives.

Professional Development

Continuous learning and professional development are essential for watercraft operators to remain updated on industry advancements and best practices. They attend training programs, workshops, and seminars to enhance their skills in navigation, safety, customer service, and environmental stewardship. Professional certifications and endorsements highlight their dedication to excellence and proficiency in their field.

Chapter 37. Wildlife Park Safari Drivers

Wildlife park safari drivers play a pivotal role in connecting visitors with nature, fostering conservation awareness, and promoting sustainable tourism practices. Their dedication to wildlife expertise, safety, guest engagement, and environmental stewardship ensures memorable and meaningful safari experiences. Safari drivers embody the spirit of adventure and conservation, making a positive impact on wildlife conservation efforts and inspiring a new generation of nature enthusiasts.

Responsibilities and Duties

Wildlife park safari drivers are entrusted with the responsibility of guiding visitors through wildlife parks and reserves, offering informative and memorable experiences. They navigate designated safari routes while ensuring the safety and comfort of guests and wildlife alike. Safari drivers adhere to park regulations, emphasizing conservation ethics and minimizing disturbances to natural habitats.

Wildlife Expertise and Interpretation

Safari drivers possess extensive knowledge of local flora and fauna, animal behavior, and ecological systems within the wildlife park. They provide engaging commentary, educating visitors about wildlife conservation efforts, endangered species, and the significance of biodiversity preservation. Their expertise enhances the safari experience, fostering appreciation for the natural environment.

Vehicle Operations and Safety

Operating safari vehicles requires proficiency in off-road driving techniques and vehicle maintenance. Safari drivers prioritize safety by conducting pre-trip inspections, ensuring vehicles are equipped with essential safety gear, and maintaining communication with park authorities. They navigate challenging terrain with skill and caution, promoting a smooth and secure safari adventure for guests.

Guest Engagement and Customer Service

Safari drivers interact with guests, offering personalized attention and enriching their safari journey. They communicate park rules, wildlife viewing etiquette, and safety protocols effectively, enhancing guest understanding and enjoyment. Safari drivers respond to guest inquiries, provide insights into wildlife behavior, and create a welcoming atmosphere conducive to learning and exploration.

Environmental Conservation

Promoting environmental stewardship is integral to the role of safari drivers. They advocate for sustainable tourism practices, educating guests on minimizing their environmental footprint and respecting wildlife habitats. Safari drivers support conservation initiatives and contribute to wildlife research efforts, playing a crucial role in preserving biodiversity and promoting ecological balance within the park ecosystem.

Emergency Preparedness

Safari drivers are trained in emergency response procedures, including first aid and vehicle rescue protocols. They maintain vigilance during safaris, anticipating potential risks and taking proactive measures to ensure guest safety. Safari drivers collaborate closely with park rangers and staff to manage emergencies swiftly and effectively, safeguarding both visitors and wildlife.

Cultural and Educational Enrichment

In addition to wildlife expertise, safari drivers share cultural insights and local knowledge with guests, offering a holistic safari experience. They highlight cultural heritage, traditional practices, and community initiatives related to wildlife conservation. Safari drivers facilitate meaningful connections between guests and the natural world, fostering appreciation for diverse cultures and ecosystems.

Professional Development
Continual learning and professional development are essential for safari drivers to enhance their skills and knowledge. They participate in training programs, workshops, and conservation seminars to stay updated on wildlife research, environmental policies, and tourism trends. Safari drivers strive for excellence in their role, contributing to the sustainable management and educational mission of wildlife parks.

The End.

www.ingramcontent.com/pod-product-compliance
Lightning Source LLC
Chambersburg PA
CBHW071923210526
45479CB00002B/525